YA 70° ⌐⌐ ⌐⌐⌐
Top 1

D1483316

PEOPLE YOU SHOULD KNOW

TOP 101 ARTISTS

Edited by Shalini Saxena

Britannica
Educational Publishing

IN ASSOCIATION WITH

ROSEN
EDUCATIONAL SERVICES

Published in 2014 by Britannica Educational Publishing (a trademark of Encyclopædia Britannica, Inc.) in association with The Rosen Publishing Group, Inc.
29 East 21st Street, New York, NY 10010

Distributed exclusively by Rosen Publishing.
To see additional Britannica Educational Publishing titles, go to rosenpublishing.com

First Edition

Britannica Educational Publishing
J.E. Luebering: Director, Core Reference Group
Anthony L. Green: Editor, Compton's by Britannica

Rosen Publishing
Hope Lourie Killcoyne: Executive Editor
Shalini Saxena: Editor
Nelson Sá: Art Director
Brian Garvey: Designer, Cover Design
Cindy Reiman: Photography Manager
Amy Feinberg: Photo Researcher

Library of Congress Cataloging-in-Publication Data

Top 101 artists / [editor] Shalini Saxena. — First edition.
     pages cm. — (People you should know)
Includes bibliographical references and index.
ISBN 978-1-62275-129-7 (library bound)
  1. Artists—Biography—Dictionaries, Juvenile. I. Saxena, Shalini, 1982- editor.
N42.T67 2014
709.2'2—dc23
[B]

                                                    2013033325

Manufactured in the United States of America

On the cover: (Top row, left to right) Michelangelo *Georgios Kollidas/Shutterstock.com*; Frida Kahlo *Archive Photos/Getty Images*; Shepard Fairey *Helga Esteb/Shutterstock.com*; Claude Monet *Hulton Archive/Getty Images*. (Bottom row, left to right) Pablo Picasso *Apic/ Hulton Archive/Getty Images*; Andy Warhol *Hulton Archive/Getty Images*; Paul Cézanne *Hulton Archive/Getty Images*; Titian *Imagno/Hulton Fine Art Collection/Getty Images*.

Cover and interior pages (top) © iStockphoto.com/René Mansi

CONTENTS

88

102

135

INTRODUCTION

D ating back to prehistoric times, the visual arts were one of the earliest forms of human expression and aesthetics, with art being considered by many philosophers to reflect the inner state of the artist, societal ideals of beauty, or important historical moments. While the study of aesthetics and art has always encompassed broad definitions of what should be considered art, what is clear is that the creation of a work of art entails the bringing about of a new combination of elements in the medium—such as tones in music, words in the case of literature, or paints on canvas—and the artist is the central figure behind this process of creation. In this book, the biographies of 101 of the most remarkable, innovative, and recognizable individuals in the history of Western art are presented, making the reader more familiar with the personalities that truly defined—and at times redefined—art throughout the ages.

Since antiquity, techniques such as drawing, painting, and sculpture have been used to represent the visible world in abstract renditions. The first and greatest period of classical art began in Greece about the middle of the 5th century BCE. By that time Greek sculptors had learned to represent the human form naturally and easily, in action or at rest. Nonetheless, their chief interest was in portraying gods. It was in this era that the Athenian sculptor Phidias constructed the largest statues to date. Under his direction the sculptures decorating the Parthenon were planned and executed. Some of them may have been the work of his own hand. His great masterpieces were the huge gold and ivory statue of Athena that stood within this temple and the similar one of Zeus in the temple at Olympia.

During Late Antiquity and the Middle Ages, Western art tended to reflect religious themes and imagery. Artwork commissioned by the Roman Catholic Church was intended to kindle reverence in believers, and artists were paid to create art embodying the Church's teachings. Early Christian murals, for example, portrayed an all-powerful, remote, and mysterious being, painted as a flat, formalized head or figure whose stern gaze dominated the interiors of temples, churches, and sanctuaries.

Paintings of the Last Judgment were intended to frighten believers, while subjects such as the Virgin enthroned and the Assumption sustained their faith with hopes for salvation and rewards of immortality.

It was only in the rare period of prolific genius and artistic flourishing known as the Renaissance that modern art history truly began. After centuries of stiff symbolic representation, Renaissance artists started to study nature itself and to work from the living model. New ideas of grace, harmony, and beauty were gained from the sculpture and other artistic remains of classical Greece and Rome. Presently came the discovery of better technical methods of execution—of the laws of perspective and the process of painting in oils. The result was that the art of painting burst into a glory previously unknown, and sculpture and architecture rivaled the grandeur of the ancient days.

The full flowering of Renaissance art came in the late 15th and early 16th centuries, with Raphael, the prince of painters, Leonardo da Vinci, and Michelangelo, embodiments of supreme many-sided genius. Each of these artists embodied the new spirit of a multitalented "Renaissance man," working across many genres and fields and helping to define the modern concept of the artist.

By the late 18th century, a new movement called romanticism began to emerge as a number of artists started to paint subjects that were at odds with the strict decorum and classical historical and mythological subject matter of conventional figurative art. These artists favored themes that were bizarre, pathetic, or extravagantly heroic, and they defined their images with tensely linear drawing and bold contrasts of light and shade. Romanticism spread across Europe, producing some of the 19th century's best-known names, including the French Eugène Delacroix and Jean-Auguste-Dominique Ingres, and Germany's Caspar David Friedrich.

The late 19th and early 20th centuries saw the development of modern art to accompany a general societal embrace of a wide variety of movements, theories, and attitudes marked by a tendency to reject traditional, historical, or academic forms and conventions. The resulting art was more in line with changing social, economic, and intellectual conditions. These modern movements included symbolism, cubism, futurism, expressionism, constructivism, Dada, surrealism, social realism, abstract expressionism, pop art, minimalism, and neo-expressionism.

An important contributing factor to this development was the acceptance of photography as an art form. The mechanical duplication of images and new technologies helped push the boundaries of representation. Important photographers including Thomas Eakins and Alfred Stieglitz worked to establish photography's place in the world of art.

Around the same time, one of the century's most thoughtful and unpredictable artists would emerge: Marcel Duchamp. His 1913 *Bicycle Wheel* was the first "ready-made," an artwork made of ordinary objects. Duchamp's aim was not to please the eyes but to make the viewer think about what art is and can be. Duchamp made humor a significant factor in serious art.

Other movements such as pop art continued to push the boundaries of art. Arising in the late 1950s, pop art developed as a reaction against abstract expressionism. Rather than avoiding references to mass culture, pop artists—including Andy Warhol and Roy Lichtenstein—accepted and used them: soft-drink bottles, gas stations, comic strips, billboards, airplanes, and hamburgers. This acceptance was not without question, for in using popular images in their art, pop artists both celebrated technological culture and revealed its cheapness and vulgarity. In the 21st century visual arts have taken new directions, as seen in the works of such artists as Shepard Fairey and Kara Walker.

In the long history of art, each of the aforementioned movements carried the world of art in a new direction and found new ways to make sense of the experience of life through a visual medium. This book is an engrossing glimpse into the works and lives of some of the world's greatest artists.

ANSEL ADAMS

(b. 1902–d. 1984)

American photographer Ansel Adams was well known for technical innovations and for his dramatic pictures of Western landscapes. He was a pioneer in the movement to preserve wilderness and one of the first to promote photography as an art form.

Adams was born in San Francisco, Calif., on Feb. 20, 1902. Originally a student of music, he took photographs only as a hobby until 1927. In that year he published his first portfolio, *Parmellian Prints of the High Sierras*. (Parmellian refers to the texture of mountain surfaces.) The style was pictorialist, similar to that of impressionist painting with its soft, misty images rather than detailed likenesses.

In 1930 Adams adopted the straight photography style of the United States photographer Paul Strand, whose photographs emphasized tones and sharp detail. Two years later, with another photographer, Adams formed Group f/64, an association of photographers who used large cameras and small apertures (lens openings) to capture an infinite variety of light and texture. Contact prints were rich in detail

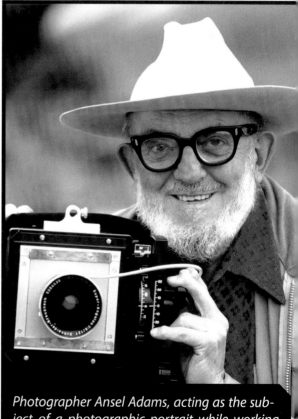

Photographer Ansel Adams, acting as the subject of a photographic portrait while working in Point Lobos, California, in the 1970s. David Hume Kennerly/Hulton Archive/Getty Images

1

and brilliant in showing tonal differences; subjects were portrayed in the most vivid way. Adams soon became one of the outstanding technicians in the history of photography. In 1935 he published *Making a Photograph*, the first of many books that he produced on photographic technique.

In 1941 Adams began making photomurals for the United States Department of the Interior. Their large scale forced him to master techniques for photographing the light and space of immense landscapes. He developed what he called the zone system, a method of determining beforehand, for each part of the scene, what the final tone would be.

Throughout his career Adams worked to increase public acceptance of photography as a fine art. He felt that an artist's final product was really no different from an artistically created photograph, intended to be preserved and respected. In 1940 he helped found the world's first museum collection of photographs at the Museum of Modern Art in New York City. In 1946 he established, at the California School of Fine Arts in San Francisco, the first academic department to teach photography as a profession.

From the time of his adolescence, Adams had a serious interest in preserving the environment. From 1936 he was a director of the Sierra Club, a group founded in 1892 to preserve the scenic beauty of particular areas in the United States. Many of Adams's books are pleas for the preservation of nature: *My Camera in the National Parks* (1950), *This Is the American Earth* (1960), and *Photographs of the Southwest* (1976). Adams also published some general photographic anthologies, including *Ansel Adams: Images, 1923–1974* (1974) and *The Portfolios of Ansel Adams* (1977). He died in 1984 in Carmel, Calif.

LEON BATTISTA ALBERTI

(b. 1404–d. 1472)

Humanist, architect, and principal initiator of Renaissance art theory, Italian Leon Battista Alberti is considered a typical example of the Renaissance "universal man." He belonged to a wealthy merchant-banker family from Florence and, at the age of 10 or 11, was sent to boarding school in Padua. There Alberti was given a classical Latin training, and he emerged as an accomplished writer.

Alberti wrote a Latin comedy at the age of 20 that was acclaimed as the "discovered" work of a Roman playwright—and was still published more than 100 years later as a Roman work. He completed his formal education at the University of Bologna, receiving his doctorate in church law in 1428.

Alberti then accepted a position as a secretary rather than pursue a legal career. By 1432 he was a secretary in the Papal Chancery in Rome. He took holy orders, and though he was known to lead an exemplary life, there is almost nothing in his subsequent career indicating that Alberti was a churchman. His interests and activities were wholly secular, and he issued an impressive series of humanistic and technical writings.

The treatise *Della Famiglia* ("On the Family"), which he began in Rome in 1432, is the first of several dialogues on which his reputation as a thinker and writer largely rests. He wrote these in the vernacular, the language of the people.

Traveling with the papal court to Florence, Alberti established close associations with the sculptor Donatello and the architect Filippo Brunelleschi. These relationships led to one of his major achievements: the book *De Pictura* ("On Painting"), which was published in 1435 and which set forth for the first time the rules for drawing a three-dimensional scene on a flat surface. It had a major effect on Italian painting and relief work, giving rise to the ordered space that became typical of the Renaissance style.

His friendship with the Florentine cosmographer Paolo Toscanelli resulted in a small treatise on geography, the first work of its kind since antiquity. It sets forth the rules for mapping a land area, and was probably as influential as his earlier treatise on painting.

At the ducal court of Este in Ferrara, where Alberti was first made welcome in 1438, he was encouraged (and commissioned) to direct his talents toward architecture. Alberti's earliest effort at reviving classical forms of building was a miniature triumphal arch in Ferrara. He began to study the architectural and engineering practices of antiquity and by 1447 was knowledgeable enough to become the architectural adviser to Pope Nicholas V.

His collaboration with the pope resulted in the first large-scale building projects of Renaissance Rome, beginning among other works the reconstruction of St. Peter's and the Vatican Palace. His long study of Vitruvius resulted in his *De re aedificatoria* ("Ten Books on Architecture"), published in 1452, not a restored text of Vitruvius but a wholly new work that won him a reputation as the "Florentine Vitruvius" and that became a bible of Renaissance architecture.

During the final 20 years of his life, Alberti carried out his architectural ideas in several outstanding buildings. The facades of Santa Maria Novella and the Palazzo Rucellai, both in Florence, are noted for their proportions. The new sense of space, which is notable in the majestic church of Sant'Andrea in Mantua, announced the fullness of the High Renaissance style. In addition to being the foremost theorist of Renaissance architecture, Alberti had become one of its great practitioners.

Although Alberti traveled to various cities and courts of Renaissance Italy, Rome and Florence remained his intellectual homes. He produced two highly original works: the first on Italian grammar, in which he demonstrated that the Tuscan vernacular was as "regular" a language as Latin and hence worthy of literary use, and a pioneer work in the writing of secret codes. His final and his finest dialogue was written in Florence in Tuscan prose. Called *De iciarchia* ("On the Man of Excellence and Ruler of His Family"), it represents in its fullness the public-spirited humanism of the earlier age to which he belonged. Alberti died in Rome "content and tranquil," according to his 16th-century biographer, Giorgio Vasari, leaving behind him "a most honorable name."

ALESSANDRO ALGARDI

(b.1595–d. 1654)

Alessandro Algardi was one of the most important Roman sculptors of the 17th century working in the Baroque style.

Algardi, the son of a silk merchant from Bologna, was born in the Papal States in Italy. He was trained under Lodovico Carracci at the Accademia degli Incamminati, where he acquired the skills of a first-rate designer. After a short period of activity in Mantua (1622), he moved to Rome (1625), where he designed the stucco decorations in San Silvestro al Quirinale and gained some success as a restorer of classical sculptures. With the monument of Cardinal Millini (d. 1629) in Santa Maria del Popolo, the Frangipani monument in San Marcello al Corso, and the bust of Cardinal Laudivio Zacchia in Berlin, Algardi emerged as the principal rival of Gian Lorenzo Bernini in the field of portrait sculpture. Lacking Bernini's dynamic vitality and penetrating characterization, Algardi's portraits were appreciated for their sobriety and surface realism.

Algardi's close association with Pietro da Cortona helped establish his reputation in Rome and also familiarized him with a classically influenced style in sculpture that owed a great deal to Roman attitudes toward historical accuracy in addition to the influence of Christian archaeology. Perhaps his most important commission in the 1630s was for the marble tomb of Pope Leo XI in St. Peter's (1644; erected 1652). Algardi emphasized Leo's largesse with allegorical figures of open-handedness and generosity of spirit as well as the relief sculpture *Cardinal de' Medici's Legation to France*. Unlike Bernini's tomb for Pope Alexander VII, which combined white and colored marble with bronze, Algardi's papal tomb was sculpted entirely from white marble.

After the election of Pope Innocent X (1644), Algardi superseded Bernini in papal favor. Between this date and his death in 1654, Algardi produced some of his most celebrated works, among them the seated statue of the pope now in the Palazzo dei Conservatori (1645) and a colossal marble profile of the *Meeting of Attila and Pope Leo* in St. Peter's (1646–53), which influenced the development and popularization of illusionistic—using perspective to add dimension to flat surfaces—reliefs. Generally less theatrical than Bernini, Algardi in this work effectively created a larger than life-size narrative whose principal events are dramatically conveyed. With his gesture of pushing away Attila, Leo points to the miraculously airborne Saints Peter and Paul, who have come to lend divine assistance. The deep shadows, emphatic gestures, and heavy drapery patterns create an arresting and convincing sense of papal power. At this time Algardi also designed the Villa Doria Pamphili and a fountain in the Cortile di San Damaso of the Vatican.

Algardi's style is less exuberant and pictorial than Bernini's, and, even in such typically Baroque works as the tomb of Pope Leo XI in St. Peter's (1634–52) and the high altar of San Paolo at Bologna (1641), the restraining influence of the antique is strongly evident. Algardi died in 1654 in Rome.

FRA ANGELICO

(b. 1400?–d. 1455)

Called *angelico* (angelic) because of his moral virtues, the monk Fra Angelico was also a great painter who combined the best of the austere Gothic tradition with the spontaneity and brightness of the Italian Renaissance. His works have been praised both for their religious qualities and for their artistic excellence.

Born Guido di Pietro at Vicchio near Florence, Italy, he had already gained a reputation as a painter by 1417. He was probably trained by Lorenzo Monaco, the greatest painter and miniaturist of the Gothic tradition. In about 1421, he entered the Dominican monastery at Fiesole, taking the name Fra (brother) Giovanni da Fiesole. Most of his life was spent there and in Florence at the monastery of San Marco. He also lived briefly in Cortona and in Rome.

Among the works he executed in Florence are *Deposition* in the church of the Holy Trinity, the *Last Judgment* and *The Coronation of the Virgin* now in the Uffizi Museum, the *Lamentation* altarpiece for the Brotherhood of Santa Maria della Croce al Tempio, and the *Annunciation* altarpiece now in a museum in Cortona. During the period 1439 to 1445, while at San Marco, Fra Angelico did most of his mural work and the magnificent altarpiece for the church of San Marco. His murals for the walls of the monastery were the high point in his career. In the chapter hall he executed a large Crucifixion scene, and in one corridor he painted a large *Annunciation* based on a similar work in Cortona. In 20 of the cells at the monastery, he and his students painted smaller Crucifixion scenes on the walls.

From 1445 to 1450 Fra Angelico worked in Rome, under the sponsorship of popes Eugene IV and Nicholas V, doing frescoes in St. Peter's

Basilica and in the chapel of the Sacrament in the Vatican. These works have all been destroyed, but his paintings for the chapel of Nicholas V are still extant. In the summer of 1447 Angelico took time out to go to Orvieto to decorate the chapel of St. Brizio in the cathedral. This work was only partly completed by him. It was continued 50 years later by Luca Signorelli.

Angelico returned to Florence in about 1450 to take on his responsibilities as prior of the monastery of San Domenico in nearby Fiesole. His most important work in this period was a cycle of 35 paintings of scenes from the life of Christ. His authorship of most of these paintings is in dispute. Many of them were probably done by his students. But three of them, *Massacre of the Innocents*, *Flight into Egypt*, and *Presentation in the Temple*, are probably his work. For the monastery of Bosco ai Frati he did an altarpiece, now in the Museum of San Marco in Florence, which was his last major work.

Angelico died in Rome on Feb. 18, 1455, in the Dominican monastery. He was buried in the church of Santa Maria della Minerva.

BENEDETTO ANTELAMI
(b. 1150–d. 1230)

Benedetto Antelami was an Italian sculptor and architect considered to have been one of the greatest of his time.

Little is known of his life. Antelami was probably born in Lombardy in Italy. It is believed that he served his apprenticeship in sculpture at Saint-Trophîme in Arles, France, and that this service may have influenced his sensitivity to French (particularly Provençal) stylistic developments. It is thought that he also belonged to the *magistri Antelami*, a civil builders' guild located in the Lake Como region of present-day northern Italy.

One of Antelami's earliest signed works is the *Deposition from the Cross*, a sculpture (dated 1178) located in the right transept of the cathedral of Parma. Between 1188 and 1218 he worked on various sculptural and architectural elements of the cathedral of Borgo San Donnino (now Fidenza) near Parma. In 1196 he started work on the construction and decoration of a portion of the magnificent baptistery of

Parma cathedral (completed 1270). Antelami's last work is believed to have been the decoration and (at least in part) the construction of the church of Sant'Andrea at Vercelli, the architecture of which successfully combined Tuscan Romanesque with Gothic characteristics (such as flying buttresses, rose windows, and ribbed vaulting) and won him lasting renown. He died in 1230 in Parma.

RICHARD AVEDON

(b. 1923–d. 2004)

As one of the leading photographers of the mid-20th century, Richard Avedon was particularly noted for his ability to capture his sitters' personalities on film. Although Avedon was best known for his fashion photography and his portraits of well-known people, he also produced fine work documenting the civil rights and antiwar movements of the 1960s.

Richard Avedon was born in New York City on May 15, 1923. He began experimenting with photography at the age of ten and immediately found that he was most interested in making portraits. His first sitter was the Russian pianist-composer Sergei Rachmaninoff, who lived in the same New York City apartment building as Avedon's grandparents.

As a young man, Avedon studied photography in the United States merchant marine and at the New School for Social Research. He turned professional in 1945 and was a regular contributor to the fashion magazine *Harper's Bazaar* from 1946 to 1965. Later he became a photographer for *Vogue* (1966–90) and for *The New Yorker* (from 1992).

Avedon's fashion photographs are characterized by a strong black-and-white contrast that creates a starkly sophisticated effect. Empty, white backgrounds and confrontational poses dramatize the personalities of celebrities and others who have sat for an Avedon portrait. Many of his photographs are collected in *Observations* (1959), with a text by Truman Capote; *Nothing Personal* (1976), with a text by James Baldwin; *Portraits* (1976); *Avedon: Photographs, 1947–1977* (1978); *In the*

Photographer Richard Avedon (on the floor), during a shoot with British model Jean Shrimpton in the 1960s. Hulton Archive/Getty Images

American West (1985); *An Autobiography* (1993); *Evidence: 1944–1994* (1994); and *The Sixties* (1999), with a text by Doon Arbus (daughter of photographer Diane Arbus). Avedon also directed a number of special television programs and served as visual consultant for the motion picture *Funny Face* (1957), starring Fred Astaire, which was based on Avedon's own experiences. Retrospective exhibitions of Avedon's photographs were mounted in 1994 by the Whitney Museum of American Art and in 2002 by the Metropolitan Museum of Art. He died on Oct. 1, 2004, in San Antonio, Texas.

GIAN LORENZO BERNINI

(b. 1598–d. 1680)

Perhaps the greatest sculptor of the 17th century and one of its outstanding architects, Gian Lorenzo Bernini created the baroque style of sculpture. He developed it to such an extent and it became so admired and popular that it continued for at least two more generations in various parts of Europe, and served as a basis for 18th-century Italian sculpture.

Gian Lorenzo Bernini was born at Naples, Italy, on Dec. 7, 1598, the son of a sculptor. He was recognized early as a prodigy. Influenced by his studies of classical Greek and Roman artworks and of High Renaissance painting, he became an architect and painter as well as a sculptor. His early works attracted the attention of Cardinal Scipione Borghese, a member of the reigning papal family.

He later received the patronage of Popes Urban VIII, Innocent X, and Alexander VII. Carrying out his belief that religious art should encourage piety, he built the immense gilt-bronze baldachin (canopy) over the tomb of St. Peter, and later St. Peter's throne behind it, in St. Peter's basilica in Rome. His major architectural achievement was also at St. Peter's, the huge oval colonnade enclosing the piazza.

The greatest single example of Bernini's mature art is usually considered to be the Cornaro Chapel in the church of Santa Maria della Vittoria in Rome. The focal point is the sculpture *The Ecstasy of St. Teresa*, depicting Teresa of Avila.

Other works include campaniles (bell towers), tombs, and fountains. His *Fountain of the Four Rivers* in Rome's Piazza Navona supports an ancient Egyptian obelisk over a hollowed-out rock surmounted by four marble figures symbolizing the four major rivers of the 17th-century world: the Danube, Nile, Ganges, and Rio de la Plata.

Bernini died in Rome on Nov. 16, 1680, after serving eight popes. At the time of his death he was widely considered one of Europe's greatest men.

HIERONYMUS BOSCH

(b. 1450?–d. 1516)

Dutch painter Hieronymus Bosch's works are full of fantastic figures, expressions of the medieval belief in witchcraft and demons. Bosch specialized in religious allegories and satirical treatments of themes from everyday life. Despite a pessimism and stern morality, he influenced many later artists through his mastery of delicate tones and his loose, rapid, direct style. His work marked the end of medieval painting.

Bosch was born Jerome van Aken in about 1450 in 's-Hertogenbosch, now in the Netherlands. He joined a religious brotherhood in 1486 and for the rest of his life took an active part in the affairs of the Confraternity of Our Lady.

His fame spread, and in 1506 he was paid for his *Last Judgment*, painted for the king of Castile (Spain). A fragment in Munich, Germany, is thought to be a part of the lost painting. A *St. Anthony* by Bosch is listed in a 1516 inventory of the collection

The central panel of The Adoration of the Magi altarpiece, an early work by Dutch painter Hieronymus Bosch. DEA/G. Dagli Orti/De Agostini/Getty Images

11

of the king's sister. Accounts of the time also mention some Bosch works in Venetian collections.

Of the 40 paintings attributed to Bosch, seven are signed but none dated. Bosch initially dealt with traditional subjects in rough, clumsy works such as the *Crucifixion*. Later he painted great panoramic triptychs, or three-paneled paintings, that provided glimpses into a hellish pandemonium. Examples are *The Temptation of St. Anthony* and *The Garden of Earthly Delights*. In his later works he changed radically, painting dense groups of half-length figures that seem to be crowding forward out of the picture. Typical of these is *The Crowning with Thorns*, in which four executioners surround Jesus. Although first recognized as an inventor of seeming nonsense, Bosch demonstrated insight into the depths of the mind and an ability to depict symbols of life and creation. Bosch died in 's-Hertogenbosch in 1516.

CONSTANTIN BRANCUSI

(b. 1876–d. 1957)

The Romanian artist Constantin Brancusi was a simple man, and this simplicity is reflected in his sculptures. They do not represent natural objects so much as they embody the spirit and essence of those objects.

Constantin Brancusi was born of a peasant family in Hobitsa, in southern Romania, on Feb. 21, 1876. He left home at an early age and worked at various crafts, including cabinetmaking. He studied at the School of Fine Arts in Bucharest from 1898 to 1902. There he made a sculpture of a man, showing the entire muscular structure. It was so exact that the school bought it to use in teaching human anatomy.

Brancusi then traveled to Munich and on to Paris, largely by walking. In Paris, though he was often too poor to eat, he studied and sculpted at the École des Beaux-Arts. In 1906 the great French sculptor Rodin invited him to work in his studio, but Brancusi refused, saying, "Nothing grows well in the shade of a big tree." In later years he would refer to anatomical sculpture including those of Rodin and Michelangelo, as well as his own early works, as "beefsteak."

Brancusi combined the inherent organic quality of the material he was using with the nature of what he wanted to sculpt. His work took a good deal from folk art and primitive sculpture. He reduced objects to the simplest, most essential shapes, eliminating all unnecessary detail. This simplicity caused him trouble with the United States Customs Department in 1926, when he sent his now-famous bronze *Bird in Space* to New York City for an exhibition. Customs refused to allow the piece to enter the country as a tax-free work of art, because they claimed it did not resemble a real bird. He fought this decision in court and—with testimony from several prominent artists, critics, and collectors—won the case.

In Paris Brancusi lived a solitary life. His best friends were artists, particularly the painter Amedeo Modigliani, the poet Ezra Pound, and the composer Erik Satie. Brancusi died in Paris on March 16, 1957. His major works include bird, fish, and turtle forms, ovoid heads, and several versions of the pillarlike *Endless Column*.

BRASSAÏ

(b. 1899–d. 1984)

Brassaï was a Hungarian-born French photographer, poet, designer, and sculptor, known primarily for his dramatic photographs of Paris at night. His chosen name Brassaï is derived from his native city. He is also known as Jules Halasz.

Brassaï was born on Sept, 9, 1899, as Gyula Halász in Brassó, Transylvania, Austria-Hungary (now Romania). He trained as an artist and settled in Paris in 1924. There he worked as a sculptor, painter, and journalist and associated with such artists as Pablo Picasso, Joan Miró, Salvador Dalí, and the writer Henry Miller. Although he disliked photography at the time, he found it necessary to use it in his journalistic assignments and soon came to appreciate the medium's unique aesthetic qualities.

Brassaï's early photographs concentrated on the nighttime world of Montparnasse, a district of Paris then noted for its artists, streetwalkers, and petty criminals. His pictures were published in a successful book,

Paris de nuit (1933; *Paris After Dark*, also published as *Paris by Night*), which caused a stir because of its sometimes scandalous subject matter. His next book, *Voluptés de Paris* (1935; "Pleasures of Paris"), made him internationally famous.

When the German army occupied Paris in 1940, Brassaï escaped southward to the French Riviera, but he returned to Paris to rescue the negatives he had hidden there. Photography on the streets was forbidden during the occupation of Paris, so Brassaï resumed drawing and sculpture and began writing poetry. After World War II, his drawings were published in book form as *Trente dessins* (1946; "Thirty Drawings"), with a poem by the French poet Jacques Prévert. Brassaï turned again to photography in 1945, and two years later a number of his photographs of dimly lit Paris streets were greatly enlarged to serve as the backdrop for Prévert's ballet *Le Rendez-vous*. Many of Brassaï's postwar pictures continued the themes and techniques of his early work. In these photographs Brassaï preferred static over active subjects, but he filled even the most lifeless images with a warm sense of human life.

The Museum of Modern Art in New York City held a retrospective exhibition of Brassaï's work in 1968. His *Henry Miller, grandeur nature* (*Henry Miller: The Paris Years*) was published in 1975, and a book of his photographs entitled *The Secret Paris of the 30's* in 1976. *Artists of My Life*, a collection of his photographic and verbal portraits of well-known artists, art dealers, and friends, was published in 1982. Brassaï died July 8, 1984, near Nice, France.

ALEXANDER CALDER

(b. 1898–d. 1976)

The abstract constructions known as "stabiles" and "mobiles" were the creation of American sculptor Alexander Calder. Trained as a mechanical engineer, Calder used his background to produce these new art forms.

Alexander Calder was born near Philadelphia on July 22, 1898. His grandfather and his father were well-known sculptors, and his mother was a painter. While working as an engineer, he studied art. From 1923

View of Alexander Calder's mobile Horizontal, on display in front of the Pompidou Centre in Paris, 2011. Patrick Kovarik/AFP/Getty Images

to 1926 he was enrolled at the Art Students League in New York City. He then spent a number of years in Paris.

A troupe of animated toys known as "Calder's Circus" brought the sculptor widespread recognition in the late 1920s. These figures of circus animals and performers were made of wood, cork, and wire. By 1930 Calder's whimsical sculptures had established him as a humorist in the art world.

A visit to Dutch artist Piet Mondrian, however, changed the direction of his work. Mondrian's colorful geometric compositions inspired Calder's first stabiles—nonrepresentational constructions of whitened wire with metal disks and spheres in contrasting red, blue, and black. They were exhibited in Paris in 1931. The first exhibition of his mobiles took place there the following year. They reflected the influence of Joan Miró. Calder's early mobiles, like his toys, were driven by motor or hand crank.

Later he made mobiles that were set into motion by slight air drafts. He also painted, designed stage sets, made jewelry, and illustrated books.

Calder maintained studios in both France and Connecticut. In his later years much of his output consisted of large stabiles designed for outdoor settings. These were curved shapes of metal, welded or riveted together. Calder died in New York City on Nov. 11, 1976.

CALLIMACHUS

(5th century BCE)

The Greek sculptor Callimachus is believed to have invented the Corinthian capital (one of the three major styles of columns in Greek architecture) after noticing acanthus leaves growing around a basket placed upon a young girl's tomb. In addition, he is often credited as the originator of the running drill for boring in marble.

Callimachus lived during the 5th century BCE in Greece, perhaps in Athens. Although no sculptures by Callimachus survive in the original, he was reported to have carved the golden lamp that burned perpetually in the Erechtheum (a temple in Athens completed in 408 BCE). He was noted and criticized by his contemporaries for the overly elaborate draperies and other details in his sculptures. Viewed in this light, the elaborate carving that characterizes the Corinthian capital may well be his invention.

Callimachus has also been linked with a series of reliefs of dancing Maenads (in Greek mythology, women devoted to the god Dionysus), a Roman copy of which is now in the Metropolitan Museum of Art in New York City. These reliefs are notable for their sensuously modeled limbs set off by abundant, rippling draperies.

ANTONIO CANOVA

(b. 1757–d. 1822)

Italian sculptor Antonio Canova was one of the greatest artists of the neoclassic movement (in art, a movement that imitated the classical art of ancient Greece and Rome). His work dominated European sculpture at the end of the 18th century and the beginning of the 19th century. He was made a marquess and given the title Marchese d'Ischia for his part in retrieving Italian works of art from Paris after Napoleon's defeat.

Antonio Canova was born on Nov. 1, 1757, in Possagno, Republic of Venice (now in Italy). He was the son of a stonemason, and after the death of his father in 1761 Canova was reared by his grandfather, also a stonemason. At the age of 11 Canova went to work with the sculptor Giuseppe Bernardi (called Torretti). The boy helped his master, executed a few humble commissions on his own, and studied classical art.

Canova set up his own studio in Venice in 1775. Four years later he sculpted *Daedalus and Icarus*. It was Canova's first important work. The figures were considered so realistic that the sculptor was accused of making plaster casts from life models. In 1781 Canova moved to Rome, where he was to spend most of the rest of his life. There he became an active and influential figure in the artistic life of the city and was always willing to help young artists and find them patrons.

In 1783 Canova received an important commission for the tomb of Pope Clement XIV in the Roman church of SS. Apostoli. When displayed in 1787 crowds flocked to see it. That same year he was commissioned to produce a tomb in St. Peter's Basilica for Pope Clement XIII. The tomb, which was completed in 1792, shows a deeper understanding of classical art than his monument to Clement XIV. Subsequent tombs were increasingly neoclassic and combined restraint with sentiment.

The French invasion of Rome in 1798 sent Canova northward to work in Vienna. In 1802, at the pope's instigation, he accepted an invitation from Napoleon to go to Paris, where he became court sculptor and considerably influenced French art. In about 1807 he finished one of his most famous works, in which he shows Napoleon's sister, Pauline Borghese, reclining almost naked on a couch as *Venus Victrix*—a combination of classical goddess and contemporary portrait. In 1811 he completed two colossal statues of Napoleon, in which the emperor is shown as a heroic classical nude.

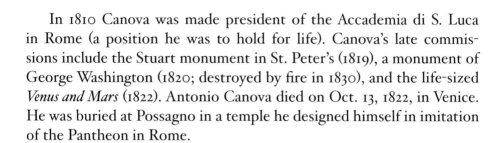

In 1810 Canova was made president of the Accademia di S. Luca in Rome (a position he was to hold for life). Canova's late commissions include the Stuart monument in St. Peter's (1819), a monument of George Washington (1820; destroyed by fire in 1830), and the life-sized *Venus and Mars* (1822). Antonio Canova died on Oct. 13, 1822, in Venice. He was buried at Possagno in a temple he designed himself in imitation of the Pantheon in Rome.

ROBERT CAPA

(b. 1913–d. 1954)

While covering the French Indochina war as a photographer for *Life* magazine, Robert Capa stepped on a land mine in Thai Binh, Vietnam, on May 25, 1954. He is believed to have been the first American killed in the Vietnam conflict. His sudden death ended the career of one of the greatest photojournalists of the 20th century.

Capa was born Andrei Friedmann in Budapest, Hungary, in 1913. As a young man he settled in Paris and established himself as a professional photographer. There he passed himself off as a wealthy American, taking the name Robert Capa.

He first gained a reputation in the 1930s as a war correspondent during the Spanish Civil War, with photographs depicting grim, close-up views of death and destruction. During World War II he covered the fighting in Africa, Sicily, and Italy for *Life* magazine. He also took memorable pictures of the Normandy invasion in June 1944. He became a U.S. citizen in 1946. After the war, in 1947, Capa was one of the founders of Magnum Photos, the first cooperative agency of international freelance photographers. He served as director of the Magnum office in Paris from 1950 to 1953.

In 1948 he photographed the fighting in the first Arab-Israeli war. He went to Vietnam to photograph the war there in 1954. Ironically, his death occurred more than two weeks after the fall of Dien Bien Phu, the battle that effectively ended the French involvement in Indochina.

CARAVAGGIO

(b. 1573?–d. 1610)

Possibly the most revolutionary artist of his time, Italian painter Caravaggio abandoned the rules that had guided a century of artists before him. He chose to paint realistically rather than idealize the human and religious experience.

He was born Michelangelo Merisi probably on Sept. 28, 1573, in Caravaggio, Italy. As an adult he would become known by the name of his birthplace. Orphaned at age 11, he was apprenticed to the painter Simone Peterzano of Milan for four years. Some time between 1588 and 1592, Caravaggio went to Rome and worked as an assistant to painters of lesser skill. About 1595 he began to sell his paintings through a dealer. The dealer brought Caravaggio to the attention of Cardinal Francesco del Monte.

Through the cardinal, Caravaggio was commissioned, at age 24, to paint for the church of San Luigi dei Francesi. In its Contarelli Chapel Caravaggio's realistic naturalism first fully appeared in three large scenes he created of the life of St. Matthew: *St. Matthew and the Angel*, *The Calling of St. Matthew*, and *The Martyrdom of St. Matthew*. The works caused public outcry, however, because of their realistic and dramatic nature. From this point he would devote himself to traditional religious themes.

Despite violent criticism, his reputation increased and Caravaggio began to be envied. He had many encounters with the law during his stay in Rome. He was imprisoned for several assaults and eventually killed an opponent after a disputed score in a game of court tennis. Caravaggio hastily fled the city and kept moving between hiding places. He reached Naples, probably early in 1607, and painted there for a time, awaiting a pardon by the pope. His works during this time include *The Seven Works of Mercy* for the Chapel of Monte della Misericordia. Here there was a shift in his painting style. The dark and urgent nature of his paintings at this time must have reflected Caravaggio's desperate state of mind.

Early in 1608 Caravaggio went to Malta and was received as a celebrated artist. Fearful of pursuit, he continued to flee for two more years, but his paintings of this time, including *The Beheading of St. John the Baptist* for the cathedral in Valletta, were among the greatest of his career. In 1610 he set sail from Naples to Rome, but he was arrested en route. After his release the boat that he was to board to continue his journey left without him, taking his belongings. Misfortune, exhaustion, and illness overtook him as he watched the boat depart. He collapsed on the beach and died a few days later on July 18, 1610.

HENRI CARTIER-BRESSON

(b. 1908–d. 2004)

Photojournalist Henri Cartier-Bresson *(foreground), working in Paris in the 1970s.*
AFP/Getty Images

With his Leica camera, French photographer Henri Cartier-Bresson traveled the world, recording the images he saw. His humane, spontaneous photographs helped establish photojournalism as an art form.

Cartier-Bresson was born in Chanteloup, near Paris, on Aug. 22, 1908. In the late 1920s he studied painting both in Paris and at Cambridge University in England. But exhibits of the photographs of Man Ray and Eugène Atget, two major 20th-century photographers, began his fascination with the camera.

In 1931 he traveled to Africa with a miniature camera. He bought his first Leica

35-millimeter camera in 1933. His first journalistic photography was in Spain during the civil war in the late 1930s. There he produced his first documentary film—on medical aid in the war. This experience stimulated an interest in motion pictures, and he worked as an assistant to the film director Jean Renoir.

During World War II Cartier-Bresson was imprisoned by the Germans, but he escaped in 1943 and joined the French underground. In 1947 he, along with Robert Capa, was a founding member of the freelance agency Magnum Photos. There were many exhibits of his work, including a 1955 traveling exhibition, before his photographs were put in the National Library in Paris. In later years most of Cartier-Bresson's interest was in motion pictures. He died on Aug. 3, 2004, in Céreste, France.

MARY CASSATT

(b. 1844–d. 1926)

Mary Cassatt, an American painter and printmaker, exhibited her works with those of the impressionists in France. She persuaded many of her wealthy American friends to buy impressionist art and thus influenced American taste in painting.

Cassatt was born in Pennsylvania on May 22, 1844. Much of her early life included traveling in Europe with her wealthy family. After attending the Pennsylvania Academy of Fine Arts in Philadelphia from 1861 to 1865, she went to Europe to study art. In Paris her work was shown in the 1874 Salon exhibit, where it was noticed by the painter Edgar Degas. Degas did not usually befriend women, but he asked Cassatt to join the impressionists—painters who used color and brushstrokes in new ways—and the two became close friends. Cassatt's work was included in impressionist exhibits in 1879, 1880, 1881, and 1886.

Her paintings were first shown on their own in Paris in 1891. Degas's influence on Cassatt is evident in her skillful drawing and in the non-centered, casual arrangement of her subjects. But her drawing is less cluttered and more precise than that of Degas. After an exhibition of Japanese prints in Paris in 1890, she began to emphasize line and

21

pattern rather than form and displayed a series of ten colored prints, or etchings, that were especially masterful. She is most famous for her pictures of mothers caring for small children, as in *The Bath*, painted about 1892.

Cassatt was important not only for the art she created but also for the art she taught people to appreciate. She collected impressionist paintings herself and encouraged her wealthy associates to do the same, speeding the acceptance of impressionism in America.

Like her friend Degas, Cassatt developed eye trouble. Her sight began to fail soon after 1900, and by 1914 she stopped painting. She died, nearly blind, on June 14, 1926, in Château de Beaufresne, near Paris.

ELIZABETH CATLETT

(b. 1915–d. 2012)

African American painter and sculptor Elizabeth Catlett was strongly influenced by the civil rights movement and dealt with economic, political, and social themes in her work. She was recognized with many prizes and honors in the United States and in Mexico.

The granddaughter of slaves, Elizabeth Catlett was born on April 15, 1915, in Washington, D.C, to a middle-class family. Her father was a professor of mathematics at Tuskegee Institute. After being disallowed entrance into the Carnegie Institute of Technology because she was black, Catlett enrolled at Howard University (B.A., *c.* 1936), where she studied design, printmaking, and drawing and was influenced by the art theories of Alain Locke and James A. Porter. She graduated with honors in 1937. While working as a muralist for two months during the mid-1930s with the Federal Art Project of the Works Progress Administration, she became influenced by the social activism of Mexican muralist Diego Rivera.

In 1940 Catlett became the first student to earn a master of fine arts degree in sculpture at the University of Iowa. Painter Grant Wood, a professor at the university at the time, encouraged her to present images drawn from black culture and experience and influenced her decision to concentrate on sculpture. After holding several teaching positions and continuing to expand her range of media, Catlett went to Mexico City in 1946 to work at the Taller de Gráfica Popular, an artists' workshop. There, along with her then husband, the artist Charles White, she created prints depicting Mexican life. As a left-wing activist, she endured investigation by the House Un-American Activities Committee during the 1950s. About 1962 she took Mexican citizenship.

Catlett is known largely for her sculpture, especially for works such as *Homage to My Young Black Sisters* (1968) and various mother-child pairings, the latter of which became

American painter and sculptor Elizabeth Catlett, attending the 2010 Jazz Interlude Gala at the Museum of Modern Art in New York City. Ben Hider/Getty Images

one of her central themes. She was also an accomplished printmaker who valued prints for their affordability and hence their accessibility to many people. Catlett alternately chose to illustrate famous subjects, such as Harriet Tubman and Malcolm X, and anonymous workers—notably, strong, solitary black women—as depicted in the terra-cotta sculpture *Negro Woman* (c. 1960) and the prints *Sharecropper* (1968) and *Survivor* (c. 1978). She remained a working artist into her 90s. Catlett died April 2, 2012, in Cuernavaca, Mexico.

PAUL CÉZANNE

(b. 1839–d. 1906)

Today many critics call Paul Cézanne the Father of Modern Painting, but during most of his life he seemed to be a failure. He sold few pictures and won no prizes. He had to be supported by his father and was also helped by the writer Émile Zola, his boyhood friend. Only in the last decade of his life was his greatness recognized.

Paul Cézanne was born in Aix-en-Provence, France, on Jan. 19, 1839. His father, Louis-Auguste, was a hatter who became a successful banker. As a child Paul was temperamental and nervous; the slightest criticism enraged him. But his family understood him, and he spent happy days wandering through the forests with young Zola and other friends.

He received a classical education at the Collège Bourbon and studied drawing at the Aix museum. After brief sessions at law school and in his father's bank, he went to Paris to study painting. Restless, he returned often to Aix. He worked many summers painting landscapes near his father's suburban home.

During the Franco-Prussian War, in 1870, Cézanne fled to Estaque, near Marseilles, to avoid becoming involved. With him went Hortense Fiquet. In 1872 their son Paul was born. Fearing disinheritance if his father learned about the child, Cézanne postponed formal marriage until Louis-Auguste died in 1886.

Cézanne took part in the first exhibition of impressionist painting in 1874, though he later broke with the impressionists. He was more concerned with structure, mass, and color than with transient effects (impressions) produced by light.

Not until Cézanne was about 60 years old did galleries and museums begin to seek out his work. Even with his newfound success he never overcame his antisocial tendencies. However, he continued to paint until a week before his death on Oct. 22, 1906.

Most 20th-century painters were influenced by Cézanne. He abandoned perspective and used overlapping planes to give objects depth. He invented a way of modeling three-dimensional forms by painting in patches of color—warm color for advancing planes, cool color for receding planes. He painted from nature but did not hesitate to distort a shape or to change its color to convey its psychological effect or to fulfill the needs of his composition. His finest works are serene but powerful expressions of forms in space.

Self-portrait by French artist Paul Cézanne. Fine Art Images/SuperStock/Getty Images

MARC CHAGALL

(b. 1887–d. 1985)

I n the whimsical world depicted by Marc Chagall, everyday objects seem to defy the laws of gravity. Cows and people float in space high above the rooftops of a distant village. Although he borrowed elements from cubism, impressionism, and fauvism, Chagall developed a style that cannot be classified with any artistic movement of his time.

One of nine children of a poor Jewish family, Chagall was born in the provincial Russian town of Vitebsk on July 7, 1887. He persuaded his reluctant parents to let him study art, first with a local teacher and then in the city of St. Petersburg. A characteristic work of this period is the nightmarish *The Dead Man*. Finally, in 1910, he set out for Paris.

There his education continued through visits to museums and galleries and contact with the painters and poets who made up the city's intellectual life. Fauvism and cubism, popular movements of the day, had some impact on his works, particularly in influencing him to use bright, clear colors, but scenes of life in Vitebsk continued to be the dominant subject matter of his art.

Chagall returned to Russia in 1914, planning a short visit. The outbreak of World War I, however, prevented him from leaving. He married Bella Rosenfeld, daughter of a wealthy Vitebsk family. The embracing lovers and bouquets of flowers that began to appear in his pictures reflect the couple's great happiness, which continued throughout their life together.

After the October Revolution in 1917 in Russia, Chagall enjoyed a brief artistic triumph as a leader of the avant-garde. As commissioner of art in Vitebsk, he organized an art academy and a museum. Later he designed stage sets at the Jewish Theater in Moscow. By 1922, however, his works had fallen into disfavor with the Soviet establishment, and Chagall decided to leave. Taking Bella and their young daughter, Ida, he returned to Paris after shortly staying in Berlin.

Chagall was idolized by the surrealists, who saw the characteristics of their own work in his 1913 *Paris Through the Window* and admired his dream imagery and the daring way he combined the figures of animals and human beings. He learned etching and did numerous book illustrations.

Chagall became equally well-known for his designs for mosaics, murals, and stained-glass windows. Among these public works are mosaics for the First National Bank plaza in Chicago; ceiling decorations for the Paris Opéra; murals for New York City's Metropolitan Opera; windows for the cathedral in Metz, France, the Art Institute of Chicago, the United Nations in New York City, and the synagogue of Hadassah-Hebrew University Medical Center in Jerusalem; and murals and tapestries for the Knesset in Jerusalem.

Except for an extended stay in the United States during the Nazi occupation of France in the 1940s, Chagall spent his mature years in France. His wife Bella died in 1944. With his second wife, Valentine, he made his home in the village of St-Paul-de-Vence on the French Riviera. He died there on March 28, 1985.

SALVADOR DALÍ

(b. 1904–d. 1989)

Despite all that was written by and about him, Spanish surrealist artist Salvador Dalí remained a mystery as a man and an artist. A curious blend of reality and fantasy characterized both his life and his works.

In the Catalonian town of Figueras, near Barcelona, Salvador Felipe Jacinto Dalí y Domenech was born on May 11, 1904. His family encouraged his early interest in art; a room in the family home was the young artist's first studio. In 1921 Dalí enrolled at the San Fernando Royal Academy of Fine Arts in Madrid. There he joined an avant-garde circle of students that included filmmaker Luis Buñuel and poet-dramatist Federico García Lorca. Although Dalí did very well in his studies, he was expelled from school because of his eccentric dress and behavior.

It was at this time that Dalí came under the influence of two forces that shaped his philosophy and his art. The first was Sigmund Freud's theory of the unconscious. The second was his association with the

Spanish surrealist painter Salvador Dalí, playing with his trademark moustache in front of one of his paintings, in 1950s London. George Konig/Hulton Archive/Getty Images

French surrealists, a group of artists and writers led by the French poet André Breton. In 1928, with the help of the Spanish painter Joan Miró, Dalí visited Paris for the first time and was introduced to the leading surrealists. The next year he settled there, becoming in a short time one of the best-known members of the group. During the 1930s his paintings were included in surrealist shows in most major European cities and in the United States.

Under the influence of the surrealist movement, Dalí's style crystallized into the disturbing blend of precise realism and dreamlike fantasy that became his hallmark. Against desolate landscapes he painted unrelated and often bizarre objects. These pictures, described by Dalí as "hand-painted dream photographs," were inspired by dreams, hallucinations, and other unconscious forces that the artist was unable to explain; they were produced by a creative method he called "paranoiac-critical activity." Dalí's most characteristic works also showed the influence of the Italian Renaissance masters, the mannerists, and the Italian metaphysical painters Carlo Carrà and Giorgio de Chirico.

During World War II Dalí and his wife, Gala, took refuge in the United States, but after the war they returned to Spain. His international reputation continued to grow, based as much on his showy lifestyle and flair for publicity as on his prodigious output of paintings, graphic works, book illustrations, and designs for jewelry, textiles, clothing, costumes, and stage sets. Dalí died in Figueras on Jan. 23, 1989.

Dalí produced two films—*An Andalusian Dog*, released in 1928, and *The Golden Age* (1930)—with Buñuel. Considered surrealist classics, they are filled with grotesque images. His writings include poetry, fiction, and a controversial autobiography, *The Secret Life of Salvador Dali* (1942). *The Persistence of Memory*, painted in 1931, is perhaps the world's most widely recognized surrealist painting.

JACQUES-LOUIS DAVID

(b. 1748–d. 1825)

French painter Jacques-Louis David is often considered the leader of the neoclassical school, which embraced the grandeur and simplicity of the art of antiquity. His works also display the seeds of the later styles of romanticism, realism, and academicism. He was the leading painter during the years of the French Revolution, but he also became the court painter of the Napoleonic empire.

David was born in Paris on Aug. 30, 1748. He entered the Royal Academy of Painting and Sculpture at age 18 and, after failing four times, won in 1774 the Prix de Rome, the much sought-after prize awarded by the government for study in Italy. In Italy David absorbed the neoclassical ideas being developed in Rome.

David returned to Paris in 1780 and was elected to the Royal Academy in 1784 for his *Andromache Mourning Hector*. His *Oath of the Horatii* created a sensation at the official Paris Salon of 1785 and immediately became the model for noble historical art. By 1789, when his *The Lictors Bringing to Brutus the Bodies of His Sons* was exhibited, the French Revolution was under way. The patriotic Roman who condemned his traitorous sons to death had unexpected political significance, and the Roman dress and furnishings shown in the picture influenced French fashion.

A member of the extremist Jacobin group led by Robespierre, David was elected in 1792 to the National Convention. He became virtually the art dictator of France, known as "the Robespierre of the brush." In that role he abolished the Royal Academy. It was during this period that he painted perhaps his greatest work, the realistic *The Death of Marat*.

After the fall of Robespierre, David was imprisoned, but he was allowed to paint, and he began what he considered his masterpiece, the giant *Sabines*. When it was exhibited in 1799, it attracted the attention of Napoleon. David again became a government painter and produced the huge *Coronation*, begun in 1805 and finished in 1807. After Napoleon's fall, David was exiled to Brussels, where he died on Dec. 29, 1825.

EDGAR DEGAS

(b. 1834–d. 1917)

The works of French impressionist artist Edgar Degas masterfully capture the human form in motion, especially female ballet dancers and bathers. Highly innovative, he found new and brilliant solutions to the problems of form, composition, and color. Degas favored pastels, but he also used a great variety of other media in his paintings, drawings, prints, and sculptures.

He was born Hilaire-Germain-Edgar de Gas, on July 19, 1834, in Paris. His father was a wealthy banker. Degas went to school at the Lycée Louis-le-Grand, then studied law. In his 20s he studied art at the École des Beaux-Arts and then traveled to Italy, where he copied the works of the old masters.

Degas's early works were historical paintings of classical subjects. In the early 1860s he began painting scenes of contemporary city life, especially at the theater, racetrack, café, and ballet. The artist Édouard Manet introduced him to impressionism. Like many future impressionists, Degas was influenced by Japanese prints and began simplifying his compositions and using lighter colors. Degas, however, preferred indoor scenes over landscapes and continued to use firm lines. Also influenced by photography, he depicted informal groupings of moving figures captured seemingly spontaneously.

In 1870 Degas served in the Franco-Prussian War. In 1874 he joined several of his artist friends in organizing the first impressionist exhibition. He also exhibited inventive works in the group's subsequent shows. He began sculpting in the 1880s.

In his later years Degas led a more closed social life but experimented boldly in his art. By 1885 his eyesight began failing, but he kept working until 1912. He died in Paris on Sept. 27, 1917.

EUGÈNE DELACROIX

(b. 1798–d. 1863)

Eugène Delacroix is numbered among the greatest and most influential of French painters. He is most often classified as an artist of the Romantic school. His remarkable use of color was later to influence impressionist painters and even modern artists such as Pablo Picasso.

Ferdinand-Victor-Eugène Delacroix was born on April 26, 1798, in Charenton-Saint-Maurice, France. In 1815 he became the pupil of the French painter Pierre-Narcisse Guérin and began a career that would produce more than 850 paintings and great numbers of drawings, murals, and other works. In 1822 Delacroix submitted his first picture to the important Paris Salon exhibition: *Dante and Virgil in Hell*. A technique used in this work—many unblended colors forming what at a distance looks like a unified whole—would later be used by the impressionists. His next Salon entry was in 1824: *Massacre at Chios*. With great vividness of color and strong emotion it pictured an incident in which 20,000 Greeks were killed by Turks on the island of Chios. The French government purchased it for 6,000 francs.

Impressed by the techniques of English painters such as John Constable, Delacroix visited England in 1825. His tours of the galleries, visits to the theater, and observations of English culture in general made a lasting impression upon him.

Between 1827 and 1832 Delacroix seemed to produce one masterpiece after another. He again used historical themes in *The Battle of Nancy* and *The Battle of Poitiers*. The poetry of Lord Byron inspired a painting for the 1827 Salon, *The Death of Sardanapalus*. Delacroix also created a set of 17 lithographs to illustrate a French edition of Goethe's *Faust*.

The French revolution of 1830 inspired the famous *Liberty Leading the People*, which was the last of Delacroix's paintings that truly embodied

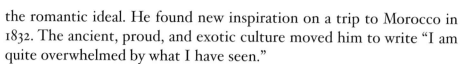

the romantic ideal. He found new inspiration on a trip to Morocco in 1832. The ancient, proud, and exotic culture moved him to write "I am quite overwhelmed by what I have seen."

In 1833 Delacroix painted a group of murals for the king's chamber at the Palais Bourbon. He continued doing this type of painting, including panels for the Louvre and for the Museum of History at Versailles, until 1861. Much of the architectural painting involved long hours on uncomfortable scaffolding in drafty buildings, and his health suffered. Delacroix died on Aug. 13, 1863, in Paris. His apartment there was made into a museum in his memory.

JEFF DONALDSON

(b. 1932–d. 2004)

Visual artist, painter, educator, and cultural activist Jeff Donaldson was central to the Black Arts Movement of the 1960s and helped develop the unique "TransAfrican" aesthetic, which drew on themes from African and African American history and culture to represent the black community.

Jeff Richardson Donaldson was born on Dec. 15, 1932, in Pine Bluff, Ark. He was raised, along with his siblings, by their mother, a school principal whose stories of race conflict inspired Donaldson. Interested in art from the time he was a child, he studied for a bachelor's degree in studio art at the University of Arkansas at Pine Bluff before going on to receive graduate degrees, including a doctorate in African and African American art history from Northwestern University.

Donaldson was at Northwestern in the late 1960s when the "black power" movement was gaining traction. At this time, he and other black artists began to explore black identity and culture through art. As part of the Organization of Black American Culture (OBAC), Donaldson and other artists were involved in creating the celebrated *Wall of Respect* in Chicago, a public mural of more than 50 prominent black leaders and figures.

Donaldson was instrumental in founding the influential African American art collective AfriCOBRA (African Commune of Bad Relevant Artists) in 1968. The members of AfriCOBRA sought to create and explore an African American aesthetic, using such visual elements as bright color, lost and found line, lettering, and more, to represent the shared history and struggles of African Americans. The aesthetic that emerged came to be known as "TransAfrican," reflecting the relationship between the social and independence movements of the United States, Africa, and the Caribbean.

Over the years Donaldson's style changed. His earlier works such as *Aunt Jemima and the Pillsbury Doughboy* (1963), *Wives of Shango* (1969), and *Victory in the Valley of Eshu* (1971) featured rich colors, figures, and symbols of traditional African and African American culture. Later works such as *JamPact JelliTite* (1988) demonstrated a more abstract style. He continued to feature political themes in his work while employing African symbols and other elements of the TransAfrican aesthetic.

Donaldson's work was displayed at solo and group shows around the world. In addition to serving as chair of Howard University's Art Department, he was also a member of the Board of Directors of the National Center for Afro-American Artists and Director of the World Black and African Festival of Art and Culture. He died in Washington D.C., on February 29, 2004.

DONATELLO

(b. 1386?–d. 1466)

One of the towering figures of the Italian Renaissance, Donatello was the greatest sculptor of the 15th century. He influenced both the realms of sculpture and painting throughout that century and beyond.

Donato (Donatello is a diminutive form) di Niccolò di Betto Bardi was born in Florence about 1386. He probably learned stone carving from one of the sculptors working on the Florence cathedral in about 1400. Between 1404 and 1407 he worked in the workshop of the Gothic sculptor Lorenzo Ghiberti, who had won the competition to create some bronze doors for the cathedral baptistery. Donatello created two marble statues—*St. Mark* and *St. George*—in a new style for the church of Or San Michele in about 1415. In these statues, for the first time since Roman classicism, the human body was shown as a functioning figure with a human personality—in sharp contrast with medieval art. Donatello's well-known statue *Zuccone* ("pumpkin" because of its bald head) of 1425 for the campanile, or bell tower, of the cathedral is a further development of the style.

For the base of *St. George* Donatello invented a totally new kind of relief, or sculpture raised from a flat surface, called *schiacciato*, meaning "flattened out." The carving was extremely shallow with details executed to catch the light in a pictorial manner rather than deeply carved figures against relatively plain backgrounds.

Donatello also worked in bronze, beginning in about 1423. The most important bronze works were *David*, the first large-scale, free-standing nude statue of the Renaissance; *Gattamelata* in Padua, the first bronze equestrian, or man-mounted-on-horse, statue to commemorate a non-ruler and the model for all subsequent equestrian monuments; and twin bronze pulpits for the Medici church of San Lorenzo in Florence, just before his death there on Dec. 13, 1466. In the late 1440s Donatello also executed a complex high altar for Padua's church of San Antonio containing seven life-size bronze statues, 21 bronze reliefs, and a large limestone relief.

MARCEL DUCHAMP

(b. 1887–d. 1968)

One of the leading spirits of 20th-century painting was the French artist Marcel Duchamp. He led the way to pop and op art with his famous cubist painting *Nude Descending a Staircase, No. 2*, through his "ready-mades," and in the movement called dadaism.

Duchamp was born in Blainville, Normandy, France, on July 28, 1887. He was one of six children, four of whom became artists. He went to Paris in 1904 and began drawing cartoons for comic books. He passed

A worker at the Scottish National Gallery in Edinburgh observes a replica of one of Marcel Duchamp's most famous and controversial pieces, *Fountain*, in 2012. Jeff J. Mitchell/Getty Images

rapidly through the then current trends in painting—postimpressionism, fauvism, and cubism—producing in 1911 *Portrait*, his first cubist painting. *Nude Descending a Staircase, No. 2* was sent to the 28th Salon des Indépendants in 1912 but was refused. The following year Duchamp sent it to the Armory Show in New York City, where it caused a scandal. It was considered a mockery of painting itself and marked the end of a serious interest in painting by the artist.

For the next 10 years Duchamp spent most of his time on an oil and lead wire construction, *The Large Glass, or The Bride Stripped Bare by Her Bachelors, Even*, which he eventually left unfinished. During that time he also produced his "ready-mades," beginning in 1913 with *Bicycle Wheel*, which was simply an ordinary bicycle wheel. He moved to New York City in 1915 and was received as a famous man. Nevertheless, he still

did not paint and devoted himself to the game of chess. He continued to be interested in surrealistic art, creating a coal sack ceiling for a 1938 exhibition in Paris and a rain room for one in 1947.

As artist and anti-artist, his entirely new attitude toward art and society, far from being negative or nihilistic, led the way to pop art, op art, and many of the other movements developed by younger artists. Not only did Duchamp change the visual arts, he also changed the mind of the artist. His 20 or so canvases and glass constructions were sold to close friends and left to the Philadelphia Museum of Art, where almost all his art is assembled. He died in Neuilly, near Paris, on Oct. 2, 1968.

ALBRECHT DÜRER

(b. 1471–d. 1528)

The son of a goldsmith, Albrecht Dürer became known as the "prince of German artists." He was the first to fuse the richness of the Italian Renaissance to the harsher northern European arts of painting, drawing, and engraving.

Albrecht Dürer was born in Nuremberg, Germany, on May 21, 1471. Before being taken into his father's shop to learn goldsmithing, he was sent to school to learn reading and writing. His talent for drawing, however, led his father to arrange an apprenticeship for him at 15 with a Nuremberg painter. After completing this apprenticeship, in 1490 Dürer visited the art centers of Germany, a tradition among young artists. In 1494, about the time of his marriage to Agnes Trey, he visited Venice. From that period on, the Italian influence was evident in his work.

Back in his home city, Dürer worked at both painting and wood engraving. Paintings were costly, and they could be enjoyed only by the purchaser and his immediate circle. By using the new craft of printing, many copies of an engraving could be made. The reproductions were used largely to educate people in religious and classical history.

In 1505 Dürer made another visit to Venice; he remained there until 1507. After his return he seems to have renounced painting as an important work and instead devoted most of his time to engraving on wood and copper. In 1513 and 1514 he completed his three best-known

copper engravings: *Knight, Death and Devil, St. Jerome in His Study*, and *Melancholia I*.

Dürer also delved into the mathematics of proportion and perspective and during his lifetime published two works on these subjects. He was a friend of Martin Luther and several other leaders of the Reformation. He died in Nuremberg on April 6, 1528.

THOMAS EAKINS

(b. 1844–d. 1916)

As has been true for so many great artists, the work of Thomas Eakins was not appreciated in his lifetime. No museum bought one of his paintings until 1916, the year he died. Nor was there a major exhibition of his work until a year later. Today he is considered one of the masters of American realism.

Thomas Eakins was born on July 25, 1844, in Philadelphia, the city where he would spend most of his life. He studied at the Pennsylvania Academy of Fine Arts, and, because of his special interest in painting the human figure, he attended lectures in anatomy at Jefferson Medical College. From 1866 to 1869 he studied in Paris at the École des Beaux-Arts (School of Fine Arts), where he gained a solid background in traditional art. He ignored all of the experimental, avant-garde work of the French impressionists and pursued his own interest in realism. After a brief visit to Spain, he returned to Philadelphia in 1870.

Eakins was a man of varied interests: painting, sculpture, anatomy, music, photography, and the study of locomotion. In the 1880s he experimented with multiple-image photography of moving animals and athletes. His interest in motion also led him to paint an impressive series of boxing scenes.

Nearly all of his work was portraiture—depictions of people he knew. His paintings demonstrated his technical expertise with external and anatomical details, combined with representations of inner character and situation. His first subjects were members of his family and an assortment of friends. Among his outdoor scenes were Max *Schmitt in a Single Scull* and *The Swimming Hole*.

37

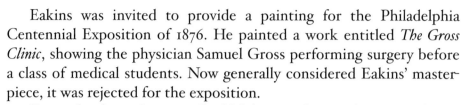
Eakins was invited to provide a painting for the Philadelphia Centennial Exposition of 1876. He painted a work entitled *The Gross Clinic*, showing the physician Samuel Gross performing surgery before a class of medical students. Now generally considered Eakins' master-piece, it was rejected for the exposition.

From the late 1870s until 1886 he taught at the Pennsylvania Academy of Fine Arts. Eventually he was forced to resign, mostly over the notoriety caused by his insistence on using live, nude models in classes of both men and women. He continued to teach from time to time at the new Art Students League and at the National Academy of Design in New York City. He died on June 25, 1916.

ENDE

(c. 10th century)

Not much is known about Ende, one of the few female artists asso-ciated with the Middle Ages. An illustrator of manuscripts, she is remembered most for her work on a group of religious texts.

The details of Ende's life remain a mystery. She was probably born and brought up in Spain in the 10th century, where she most likely trained to become a nun. Her talent for illustration in addition to her religious education made her a good choice to illustrate religious texts, a task reserved for those in religious orders. It is even possible that she was trained as an artist after joining the Church.

Ende worked on an illuminated manuscript called the *Beatus of Girona*, which contains the *Commentary on the Apocalypse* and is now housed in the Girona Cathedral. The color and symmetry of the work show influences of the bright Mozarabic style that developed after the Muslim invasion of Spain. Although the name of one of Ende's male col-leagues, Emeterius, can also be found on the manuscript, Ende's name appears on more than one work in the series, with her signature "Ende, pintrix et dei aiutrix" (sometimes read as "En depentrix and deiautrix") in Latin, which means "paintress and helper of God." It is likely that the work was a collaboration between them, with Ende's involvement appearing to be significant.

JAN VAN EYCK

(b. 1390?–d. 1441)

The Flemish painter who perfected the new technique of painting in oils, Jan van Eyck produced mostly portraits and religious subjects on wooden panels. His works often contain disguised religious symbols.

Van Eyck was probably born in Maaseik, now in Belgium, before 1395. From 1422 to 1425 he was in the service of John of Bavaria, count of Holland, in The Hague. For the rest of his life he served Philip the Good, duke of Burgundy.

Only nine of Van Eyck's paintings are signed and only ten are dated. His masterpiece, *The Adoration of the Lamb* altarpiece in Ghent's St. Bavon Cathedral, is dated 1432, but it also has a questionable 16th-century inscription that introduces Hubert van Eyck, supposedly his brother, as its principal master. There are no other references to the brother, but a "Master Hubert, the painter" is mentioned in city records.

Van Eyck moved from a heavy, sculptural realism to a more delicate pictorial style. This development can be traced most notably in *Portrait of a Young Man* (1432); *Madonna of Autun* (1433); *The Marriage of Giovanni Arnolfini and Giovanna Cenami* (1434), *Madonna with Chancellor Rolin* (1435); *Madonna with Canon van der Paele* (1436); *St. Barbara* (1437); and *Madonna at the Fountain* (1439). His paintings are known for the beauty of their colors and their special qualities of light. Said the French writer Chateaubriand when he saw the *Ghent Altarpiece*: "Where did the Flemish painters steal their light...What ray of Greece has strayed to the shores of Holland?" Van Eyck died in Brugge and was buried on July 9, 1441, in the Church of St. Donatian, which was destroyed in 1799.

SHEPARD FAIREY

(b. 1970–)

The popularity of contemporary artist Shepard Fairey exploded after the creation of his iconic *Hope* poster during Barack Obama's presidential campaign in 2008. However, the street artist, graphic designer, and illustrator had been in action long before then, combining elements from street art, graffiti, and political imagery to provoke viewers into reexamining their relationship to their surroundings and to the messages to which they are exposed.

Frank Shepard Fairey was born on Feb. 15, 1970. He was born and brought up in Charleston, South Carolina. He was producing art works through his teen years and went on to receive a bachelor's degree from the Rhode Island School of Design in 1992. In 2001 he married Amanda Alaya, a former colleague and occasional model for his work.

In 1989, while a student in college, Fairey and his friends began a campaign entitled "Andre the Giant Has a Posse," which featured stickers and prints designed by Fairey with the face of actor and wrestler André the Giant and the words "Andre the Giant Has a Posse." Fairey also altered the image and produced the stylistically different "OBEY Giant," which features a close-up rendering of André the Giant's face and the word "Obey." Although initially intended for his friends and those in the skateboarding community with which he was associated, the campaign took off and went viral, with stickers and prints appearing in various visible and public spaces. He has called the campaign an experiment in phenomenology. Like his later work, the campaign had political undertones as well as a sense of playfulness and rebellion.

Fairey continued to work with mixed media, designing T-shirts, skateboards, album covers, film posters, and more. In 2004 he created a series of "anti-war, anti-Bush" posters with other artists that were controversial for their messages and imagery. In 2008 a series of images he had designed for then U.S. presidential candidate Barack Obama were picked up by the presidential campaign and soon came to be identified with it. The poster that was most prominently featured shows a close-up of Barack Obama's head and the word "Hope." Created in the Russian constructivist style commonly seen in state propaganda campaigns, the *Hope* poster soon came to be seen as one of the symbols of the Obama campaign, catapulting Fairey to fame. With its positive message, the *Hope* poster also marked a shift away from Fairey's earlier works, which were often critical

American contemporary artist Shepard Fairey makes his mark while attending the 2013 South by Southwest (SXSW) in Austin, Texas. Vivien Killilea/Getty Images

of mainstream politics. Although legal issues later arose over Fairey's use of Obama's photograph in the poster, the image remains iconic.

In 2006 Fairey released a book of his work called *Obey: Supply and Demand*. In 2011, he designed a poster for the Occupy Wall Street movement. Although he remains controversial in many respects, Fairey continues to create thought-provoking works, many of which continue to be displayed in studios and galleries.

JOHN FLAXMAN

(b. 1755–d. 1826)

The leading artist of the neoclassical style in England was John Flaxman. A sculptor and illustrator, he was celebrated for creating memorial sculptures, including one for Admiral Horatio Nelson. Flaxman was one of the few British artists of his time with an international reputation.

Flaxman was born on July 6, 1755, in York, Yorkshire, England. As a youth he worked in his father's plaster-casting studio in London and began reading classical literature, which became a continual inspiration to him. In 1770 he entered the Royal Academy schools and formed a lifelong friendship with poet-artist William Blake, who stimulated his interest in Gothic art. After 1775 he began to work for the noted potter Josiah Wedgwood. He produced designs, usually based on antique models, for the silhouette decorations of Wedgwood's pottery; the discipline of this work strengthened Flaxman's feeling for line.

In 1787 Flaxman went to Rome to direct the Wedgwood studio there. He planned to stay just two years, but he received enough commissions for his art that he remained until 1794. His artistic beliefs were formed in those years. He drew diligently from ancient art and Italian medieval and Renaissance art, and he was determined to give his work a moral purpose. Between 1790 and 1794 he produced ambitious and relatively unsuccessful group sculptures such as *The Fury of Athamas* and *Cephalus and Aurora*. His book illustrations, in clean linear rhythms, were far more important. He became noted for his depictions of scenes from Homer's *Iliad* and *Odyssey* (1793), Aeschylus's plays (1795), and Dante's *Divine Comedy* (1802). Later he designed a volume of Hesiod's poetry that Blake engraved in 1817.

After Flaxman returned to London his designs for a large monument to the earl of Mansfield (1793–1801) established his reputation as a sculptor. He became a member of the Royal Academy in 1800 and its first professor of sculpture in 1810. The number of works he produced after 1800 was enormous. They ranged from small monuments in relief to large sculptures in the round, such as the Nelson monument in St. Paul's Cathedral (1808–18). He also made some designs for silversmiths; the most famous was "The Shield of Achilles" (1818).

Flaxman's chief strengths were his sincerity and his remarkable fertility of ideas. His designs include figures in contemporary dress as well as in the classical manner. In his own day his reputation as a sculptor rivaled the reputations of his great contemporaries Antonio Canova and Bertel Thorvaldsen. Flaxman died on Dec. 7, 1826, in London.

CASPAR DAVID FRIEDRICH

(b. 1774–d. 1840)

The vast, mysterious landscapes and seascapes of 19th-century German Romantic painter Caspar David Friedrich proclaimed man's helplessness against the forces of nature. Friedrich helped establish the idea of the sublime as a central concern of the Romantic Movement.

Friedrich was born on Sept. 5, 1774, in Greifswald, Pomerania (now Germany). He studied from 1794 to 1798 at the academy at Copenhagen but was largely self-taught. Settling at Dresden, he became a member of an artistic and literary circle that included the painter Philipp Otto Runge and the writers Ludwig Tieck and Novalis. His drawings in sepia, executed in his neat early style, won the poet Johann Wolfgang von Goethe's approval and a prize from the Weimar Art Society in 1805.

Friedrich's first important oil painting, *The Cross in the Mountains* (*c.* 1807), established his mature style. This painting was characterized by an overwhelming sense of isolation and was an attempt to replace the traditional symbols of religious painting with those drawn from nature. Other symbolic landscapes, such as *Shipwreck in the Ice* (1822), reveal a fatalism and obsession with death. Though based on close observation of nature, his works were colored by his imaginative response to the atmosphere of the Baltic coast and the Harz Mountains, which he found both awesome and ominous. In 1824 he was made professor of the Dresden academy. By the time of his death on May 7, 1840, in Dresden, his work was largely forgotten. His reputation grew, however, as 20th-century artists recognized the existential isolation in his work.

THOMAS GAINSBOROUGH

(b. 1727–d. 1788)

As a boy Thomas Gainsborough drew pictures of the English countryside near his home. Throughout his career he continued to

enjoy landscape painting. Yet he won his greatest popularity as a portrait painter.

Thomas Gainsborough was born in Sudbury, Suffolk County, England. When he was 14 his parents sent him to London as assistant to Hubert Gravelot, an illustrator and engraver. Two years later he entered St. Martin's Lane Academy. There he studied under Francis Hayman, a skillful painter of portraits and historic scenes. Gainsborough married at 19. For 14 years he lived quietly at Sudbury and Ipswich. Then he moved to Bath and began to do more portrait painting. He had immediate success. Some years later he moved to London and became a favorite painter of the royal family. He was one of the original members of the Royal Academy, which was founded in 1768, but left in 1784 after disagreements over the hanging of his paintings.

Among Gainsborough's famous landscapes are *Cornard Wood*, *The Market Cart*, *The Watering Place*, and *The Bridge*. His portraits include *Mrs. Sheridan*, *The Honorable Mrs. Graham*, *David Garrick*, *Mrs. Siddons*, *Mrs. Robinson (Perdita)*, *The Morning Walk*, and *The Duchess of Devonshire*. His full-length portrait of Jonathan Buttall is world famous as *The Blue Boy*.

During his last years Gainsborough also painted seascapes and idealized full-size pictures of rustics and country children. He died in 1788 and was buried in Kew churchyard.

PAUL GAUGUIN

(b. 1848–d. 1903)

The leading French painter of the postimpressionist period, Paul Gauguin was at his best when he could paint what he called "natural" men and women living with their fears, faiths, myths, and primitive passions. He created many of his works while living on Tahiti from 1891 to 1893 and 1895 to 1901 and the Marquesas Islands from 1901 to 1903 in the southern Pacific Ocean. Gauguin was attracted to primitivism because while working in this style he could present clearly intelligible images, use simple color harmonies, and make pictures that were decorative and pleasing to the eye.

Eugène-Henri-Paul Gauguin was born in Paris on June 7, 1848. Three years later his family moved to Lima, Peru, his mother's home. In 1855

Self-Portrait with the Yellow Christ by Paul Gauguin. DEA/G. Dagli Orti/De Agostini/Getty Images

he and his mother were back in France at Orléans. At age 17 he left home to sail around the world for six years in freighters and warships. In 1871 he went to work for a stockbroking firm in Paris. Two years later he married a young Danish woman, Mette Sophie Gad.

It was while at the business firm that he took an interest in painting. Influenced by fellow workers and friends, Gauguin developed an interest in impressionist art. He collected works by Manet, Pissarro, Monet, and others. For a time he worked with Pissarro to master the techniques of drawing and painting.

He became more absorbed in his painting after his *Landscape at Viroflay* was accepted for an exposition in 1876. In 1883 the stock market crashed, and he lost his job. For a while he and his wife lived in Denmark with her parents. In 1885 he was back in Paris alone,

determined to make a living at his art. He did not succeed. A journey to Martinique in the West Indies in 1887 introduced him to the bright colors and delights of the tropics. He also discovered primitive art, and its appeal led him to turn away from impressionism. Among the paintings for which he is justly famous are *Vision After the Sermon* (1888), *When Shall We Be Married?* (1892), *Holiday* (1896), and *Two Tahitian Women* (1899). From 1899 his health deteriorated, and he died on the Marquesas on May 8, 1903. Among the artists who learned much from Gauguin's work were Edvard Munch, Henri Matisse, and the young Pablo Picasso.

ARTEMISIA GENTILESCHI

(b. 1593–d. 1652/53)

The Italian painter Artemisia Gentileschi was also the daughter of Orazio Gentileschi, a major follower of the revolutionary Baroque painter Caravaggio. Artemisia Gentileschi was an important second-generation proponent of Caravaggio's dramatic realism.

Gentileschi was born in Rome, in the Papal States of Italy on July 8, 1593. A pupil of her father and of his friend the landscape painter Agostino Tassi, she painted at first in a style that was difficult to differentiate from her father's somewhat lyrical interpretation of Caravaggio's example. Her first known work is *Susanna and the Elders* (1610), an accomplished work long attributed to her father. She also painted two versions of a scene already essayed by Caravaggio (but never attempted by her father), *Judith Beheading Holofernes* (c. 1612–13; c. 1620). She was raped by Tassi, and, when he did not fulfill his promise to marry her, Orazio Gentileschi in 1612 brought him to trial. During that event she herself was forced to give evidence under torture.

Shortly after the trial Gentileschi married a Florentine, and in 1616 she joined Florence's Academy of Design, the first woman to do so. While in Florence she began to develop her own distinct style. Unlike many other women artists of the 17th century, she specialized in history painting rather than still life and portraiture. In Florence she was associated with the Medici court and painted an *Allegory of Inclination* (*c.* 1616) for the series of frescoes honoring the life of Michelangelo in the Casa Buonarotti. Her colors are more brilliant than her father's, and she continued to employ the tenebrism (the use of extreme contrasts of light and dark in figurative compositions to heighten their dramatic effect) made popular by Caravaggio long after her father had abandoned that style.

Artemisia Gentileschi was in Rome for a time and also in Venice. About 1630 she moved to Naples, and in 1638 she arrived in London, where she worked alongside her father for King Charles I. They collaborated on the ceiling paintings of the Great Hall in the Queen's House in Greenwich. After Orazio's death in 1639, she stayed on in London for at least several more years. According to her biographer Baldinucci (who added her life to that of her father), she painted many portraits and quickly surpassed her father's fame. Later, probably in 1640 or 1641, she settled in Naples, where she painted several versions of the story of David and Bathsheba, but little is known of the final years of her life. She is believed to have died sometime between 1652 and 1653.

GIOTTO DI BONDONE

(b. 1266?–d. 1337)

Outstanding as a painter, sculptor, and architect, Giotto was recognized as the first genius of art in the Italian Renaissance. Giotto lived and worked at a time when people's minds and talents were first being freed from the shackles of medieval restraint. He dealt largely in the traditional religious subjects, but he gave these subjects an earthly, full-blooded life and force.

The artist's full name was Giotto di Bondone. He was born about 1266 in the village of Vespignano, near Florence. His father was a small landed farmer. Giorgio Vasari, one of Giotto's first biographers, tells how Cimabue, a well-known Florentine painter, discovered Giotto's talents. Cimabue supposedly saw the 12-year-old boy sketching one of his father's sheep on a flat rock and was so impressed with his talent

Frescoes by Giotto di Bondone at the Cathedral Basilica of St. Francis in Assisi, Italy. The frescoes were painted during the Renaissance and were restored in 2010. Franco Origlia/Getty Images

that he persuaded the father to let Giotto become his pupil. Another story is that Giotto, while apprenticing to a wool merchant, frequented Cimabue's studio so much that he was finally allowed to study painting.

The earliest of Giotto's known works is a series of frescoes (paintings on fresh, still wet plaster) on the life of St. Francis in the church at Assisi. Each fresco depicts an incident; the human and animal figures are realistic and the scenes expressive of the spirit of the patron saint of animals. In about 1305 and 1306 Giotto painted a notable series of 38 frescoes in the Arena Chapel in Padua. The frescoes illustrate the lives of Jesus and Mary. Over the archway of the choir is a scene of the Court of Heaven, and a Last Judgment scene faces it on the entrance wall. The compositions are simple, the backgrounds are subordinated, and the faces are studies in emotional expression.

Vasari tells the story of how Pope Boniface VIII sent a messenger to Giotto with a request for samples of his work. Giotto dipped his brush in red and with one continuous stroke painted a perfect circle. He then assured the messenger that the worth of this sample would be recognized. When the Pope saw it, he "instantly perceived that Giotto surpassed all other painters of his time."

In Rome, Naples, and Florence, Giotto executed commissions from princes and high churchmen. In the Bargello, or Palace of the Podestà (now a museum), in Florence is a series of his Biblical scenes. Among the bystanders in the paintings is a portrait of his friend the poet Dante. The Church of Santa Croce is adorned by Giotto murals depicting the life of St. Francis.

In 1334 the city of Florence honored Giotto with the title of Magnus Magister (Great Master) and appointed him city architect and superintendent of public works. In this capacity he designed the famous campanile (bell tower). He died in 1337, before the work was finished.

Giotto was short and homely, and he was a great wit and practical joker. He was married and left six children at his death. Unlike many of his fellow artists, he saved his money and was accounted a rich man. He was on familiar terms with the pope, and King Robert of Naples called him a good friend.

As with many other artists of his day, Giotto lacked the technical knowledge of anatomy and perspective that later painters learned. Yet he had a grasp of human emotion and of what was significant in human life. In concentrating on these essentials he created compelling pictures of people under stress, of people caught up in crises and soul-searching decisions. Modern artists often seek inspiration from Giotto, finding a direct approach to human experience that remains valid for every age.

VINCENT VAN GOGH

(b. 1853–d. 1890)

One of the four great postimpressionists (along with Paul Gauguin, Georges Seurat, and Paul Cézanne), Vincent van Gogh is generally considered the greatest Dutch painter after Rembrandt. His reputation is based largely on the works of the last three years of his short ten-year painting career, and he had a powerful influence on expressionism in modern art. He produced more than 800 oil paintings and 700 drawings, but he sold only one during his lifetime. His striking colors, coarse brushwork, and contoured forms display the anguish of the mental illness that drove him to suicide.

Vincent Willem van Gogh was born on March 30, 1853, in Zundert in the Brabant region of the Netherlands. He was the eldest son of a Protestant clergyman. At the age of 16 Van Gogh was apprenticed to art dealers in The Hague, and he worked for them there and in London and Paris until 1876.

Van Gogh disliked art dealing, and, rejected in love, he became increasingly solitary. He began to prepare for the ministry, but he failed the entrance examinations for seminary and became a lay preacher. In 1878 he went to the impoverished Borinage district in southwestern Belgium to do missionary work. He was dismissed in 1880 over a disagreement with his superiors. Penniless and with his faith broken, he sank into despair and began to draw. He soon realized the limitations of being self-taught and went to Brussels to study drawing. In 1881 he moved to The Hague to work with the Dutch landscape painter Anton Mauve, and the next summer Van Gogh began to experiment with oil paints. His urge to be "alone with nature" took him to Dutch villages, and his subjects—still life, landscape, and figure—all related to the peasants' daily hardships and surroundings. In 1885 he produced his first masterpiece, *The Potato Eaters*.

Feeling too isolated, he left for Antwerp, Belgium, and enrolled in the academy there. He did not respond well to the school's rigid discipline, but while in Antwerp he was inspired by the paintings of Peter Paul Rubens and discovered Japanese prints. He was soon off to Paris, where he met Henri de Toulouse-Lautrec and Gauguin and discovered the impressionists Camille Pissarro, Seurat, and others. Van Gogh's two years in Paris shaped his personal style of painting—more colorful, less traditional, with lighter tonalities and distinctive brushwork.

Tired of city life, Van Gogh left Paris in 1888 for Arles in the south of France. He rented and decorated a yellow house in which he hoped to found a community of "impressionists of the South." Gauguin joined him in October, but their relations deteriorated, and in a quarrel on Christmas Eve Van Gogh cut off part of his own left ear. Gauguin left, and Van Gogh was hospitalized. Exhibiting repeated signs of mental disturbance, Van Gogh asked to be sent to an asylum at St-Rémy-de-Province. After a year of confinement he moved to the home of a physician-artist in Auvers-sur-Oise for two months. On July 27, 1890, Van Gogh shot himself; he died two days later.

Despite his deteriorating mental condition, Van Gogh's time at Arles, in the asylum, and at Auvers proved to be his greatest productive periods. At Arles he painted with great energy the sun-drenched fields and flowers; at St-Rémy the colors of his paintings were more muted, but the lines were bolder and the whole more visionary; in the northern light of Auvers he adopted pale, fresh tonalities, a broader and more expressive brushwork, and a lyrical vision of nature. The sale of Van Gogh's *Irises* in 1987 brought the highest price ever paid for a work of art up to that time—53.9 million dollars.

FRANCISCO DE GOYA

(b. 1746–d. 1828)

For the bold technique of his paintings, the haunting satire of his etchings, and his belief that the artist's vision is more important than tradition, Goya is often called "the first of the moderns." His uncompromising portrayal of his times marks the beginning of 19th-century realism.

Francisco José de Goya y Lucientes was born on March 30, 1746, in Fuendetodos, a village in northern Spain. The family later moved to Saragossa, where Goya's father worked as a gilder. At about 14 young Goya was apprenticed to José Luzán, a local painter. Later he went to Italy to continue his study of art. On returning to Saragossa in 1771, he painted frescoes for the local cathedral. These works, done in the decorative rococo tradition, established Goya's artistic reputation. In 1773 he married Josefa Bayeu, sister of Saragossa artist Francisco Bayeu. The couple had many children, but only one son survived to adulthood.

51

Self-portrait of Francisco de Goya, whose works are indicative of 19th-century realism. DEA/G. Nimatallah/De Agostini/ Getty Images

From 1775 to 1792 Goya painted cartoons (designs) for the royal tapestry factory in Madrid. This was the most important period in his artistic development. As a tapestry designer, Goya did his first genre of paintings, or scenes from everyday life.

The experience helped him become a keen observer of human behavior. He was also influenced by neoclassicism, which was gaining favor over the rococo style. Finally, his study of the works of Velázquez in the royal collection resulted in a looser, more spontaneous painting technique.

At the same time, Goya achieved his first popular success. He became established as a portrait painter to the Spanish aristocracy. He was elected to the Royal Academy of San Fernando in 1780, named painter to the king in 1786, and made a court painter in 1789.

A serious illness in 1792 left Goya permanently deaf. Isolated from others by his deafness, he became increasingly occupied with the fantasies and inventions of his imagination and with critical and satirical observations of mankind. He evolved a bold, free new style close to caricature. In 1799 he published the *Caprichos*, a series of etchings satirizing human folly and weakness. His portraits became penetrating characterizations, revealing their subjects as Goya saw them. In his religious frescoes he employed a broad, free style and an earthy realism unprecedented in religious art.

Goya served as director of painting at the Royal Academy from 1795 to 1797 and was appointed first Spanish court painter in 1799. During the Napoleonic invasion and the Spanish war of independence from 1808 to 1814, Goya served as court painter to the French. He expressed his horror of armed conflict in *The Disasters of War*, a series of starkly realistic etchings on the atrocities of war. They were not published until 1863, long after Goya's death.

Upon the restoration of the Spanish monarchy, Goya was pardoned for serving the French, but his work was not favored by the new king. He was called before the Inquisition to explain his earlier portrait of *The Naked Maja*, one of the few nudes in Spanish art at that time.

In 1816 he published his etchings on bullfighting, called the *Tauromaquia*. From 1819 to 1824 Goya lived in seclusion in a house outside Madrid. Free from court restrictions, he adopted an increasingly personal style. In the *Black Paintings*, executed on the walls of his house, Goya gave expression to his darkest visions. A similar nightmarish quality haunts the satirical *Disparates*, a series of etchings also called *Proverbios*.

In 1824, after the failure of an attempt to restore liberal government, Goya went into voluntary exile in France. He settled in Bordeaux, continuing to work until his death there on April 16, 1828. Today many of his best paintings hang in Madrid's Prado art museum.

GRANDMA MOSES

(b. 1860–d. 1961)

A merican artist Grandma Moses was a self-taught primitive artist and folk painter. In her later years she became internationally popular for her naïve documentation of rural life in the United States in the late 19th and early 20th centuries.

Anna Mary Robertson was born on Sept. 7, 1860, in Greenwich, N.Y. She had only short periods of schooling during her childhood. At age 12 she left her parents' farm and worked as a hired girl until she married Thomas Moses in 1887. The couple first farmed in the Shenandoah Valley near Staunton, Virginia, but in 1905 moved to a farm

American folk artist Anna Mary Robertson Moses, known as Grandma Moses, at work on a sketch in the 1950s. Archive Photos/ Getty Images

at Eagle Bridge, N.Y., near the place where Anna had been born. Thomas died in 1927, and Anna continued to farm with the help of her youngest son until advancing age forced her to retire to a daughter's home in 1936.

As a child Moses had drawn pictures and colored them with the juice of berries and grapes. After her husband died she created worsted embroidery pictures, and, when her arthritis made manipulating a needle too difficult, she turned to painting. At first she copied illustrated postcards and Currier & Ives prints, but gradually she began to re-create scenes from her childhood, as in *Apple Pickers* (*c.* 1940), *Sugaring-Off in the Maple Orchard* (1940), *Catching the Thanksgiving Turkey* (1943), and *Over the River to Grandma's House* (*c.* 1944). Her early paintings were given away or sold for small sums. In 1939 several of her paintings hanging in a drugstore window in Hoosick Falls, N.Y., impressed Louis Caldor, an engineer and art collector, who then bought her remaining stock of 15 paintings. In October of that year three of those paintings were exhibited at the Museum of Modern Art in New York City in a show entitled "Contemporary, Unknown Painters."

From the beginning Grandma Moses's work received favorable criticism. In October 1940 a one-woman show of 35 paintings was held at Galerie St. Etienne in New York City. Thereafter her paintings were shown throughout the United States and Europe in some 150 solo shows and 100 group exhibits. Throughout her lifetime Grandma Moses produced about 2,000 paintings, most of them on Masonite board. Her naïve style (labeled American Primitive) was acclaimed for its purity of color, its attention to detail, and its vigor. Her other notable paintings include *Black Horses* (1942), *Out for the Christmas Trees* (1946), *The Old Oaken Bucket* (1946), *From My Window* (1949), and *Making Apple Butter* (1958). From 1946 her paintings were often reproduced in prints and on Christmas cards. Her autobiography, *My Life's History*, was published in 1952. Grandma Moses died on Dec. 13, 1961, in Hoosick Falls.

EL GRECO

(b. 1541–d. 1614)

For centuries the vibrant colors, unusual perspectives, and strangely contorted figures of El Greco's paintings were widely misunderstood. While some critics attributed these characteristics to a defect in the artist's eyesight, others saw them as an expression of El Greco's unique artistic vision.

Not much is known of El Greco's early life, his family, or his artistic training. By his own testimony, Domenikos Theotokopoulos was born about 1541 in Iráklion on the island of Crete. In 1570, the first documented date in his life, he arrived in Rome already an accomplished artist. According to Roman contemporaries he had come from Venice, where he had studied the works of Titian, Tintoretto, and Bassano, and may even have been a pupil of Titian. Paintings of El Greco's Roman period show the influence of the Venetian masters, the Italian mannerists, and the late works of Michelangelo. In Italy he was nicknamed "The Greek," or "El Greco" (actually *Il Greco* in Italian), the name by which he became known.

When and why El Greco went to Spain is unknown. He is thought to have arrived there in 1576, when he was commissioned to design and paint the altarpieces for a church in Toledo. During the same time, he painted the *Espolio* (*Disrobing of Christ*) for the Toledo cathedral. His high price for this work involved him in the first of many lawsuits, and church authorities demanded that he modify his unconventional

treatment of the subject. His *Martyrdom of Saint Maurice and the Theban Legion*, commissioned by King Philip II, was not favorably received, thus ending El Greco's hopes of royal patronage.

El Greco settled permanently in the town of Toledo, a center of religious and cultural activity. From 1577 until his death he was much in demand as a painter of religious scenes and a designer of altarpieces, or retables. Although a majority of his commissions were for religious works, he also painted a number of portraits and some dramatic views of the Toledo landscape. The characteristic style of El Greco's works became fully mature after his arrival in Spain. It combined his Byzantine heritage, his Italian training, and his experience of Spain's fervent religious atmosphere.

The Burial of the Conde de Orgaz, which El Greco completed in 1588, is generally considered his masterpiece. The painting vividly depicts the contrast between heaven and Earth. In its grouping of extraordinary portraits are tall, phantomlike saints with distorted forms and contemporary figures with normal scale and proportions.

Little is known of El Greco's personal life. His companion in Toledo was Doña Jerónima de las Cuevas, the mother of his son, Jorge Manuel, who was born in 1578. He was a respected member of the community, admired for his knowledge and talents. Plagued during his later years by ill health and debts, he died in Toledo on April 7, 1614.

MATTHIAS GRÜNEWALD

(b.?–d. 1528)

For more than 350 years after his death, the outstanding German painter Matthias Grünewald was almost forgotten. Even today nothing is known of his early life. It is believed that he was almost 50 years old in 1519, which would mean he was born about 1470, probably in Würzburg, Germany. His name first appears in documents from either the town of Seligenstadt or from Aschaffenburg, to the northwest of Würzburg. His real name was Mathis Gothardt. Grünewald was mistakenly given to him by his 17th-century biographer, Joachim von Sandrart.

In about 1509 Grünewald became court painter for the archbishop of Mainz. Most of his paintings and drawings were of a religious nature. He is known for a number of *Crucifixions*, depictions of the Virgin Mary, and an assortment of saints. The most significant assignment of his career was the execution of a series of painted panels for the altar of a monastery in Isenheim, Alsace (now in northeastern France). He also painted the high altar for the church of Saints Peter and Alexander in Aschaffenburg from 1517 to 1519.

From 1514 to 1526 Grünewald worked for Albrecht of Brandenburg, who was both prince and cardinal, painting for him the luxurious *Saints Erasmus and Mauritius*. He spent the last two years of his life visiting Halle and Frankfurt.

It is probable that Grünewald became sympathetic to the teachings of Martin Luther during this period. After his death at Halle in August 1528, a number of Lutheran documents and pamphlets were found among his possessions.

HANS HOLBEIN, THE YOUNGER

(b. 1497–d. 1543)

An influential German family of artists of the late 15th and early 16th centuries was the Holbein family. Its most famous member, Hans the Younger, is best known for the realistic portraits he painted of the court of King Henry VIII of England. Other painters in the family were Hans the Younger's father, Hans the Elder; uncle, Sigmund; and brother, Ambrosius.

Born in Augsburg, Bavaria, Hans received his first lessons in art from his father. In 1515 the younger Holbein went to Basel, Switzerland, with his brother, Ambrosius. Among the many scholars living in Basel at that time was the famous Dutch humanist Erasmus, who befriended the young artist and asked him to illustrate his satire, *Encomium Moriae* ("The Praise

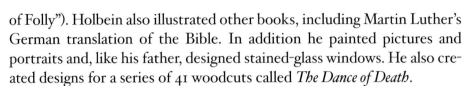

of Folly"). Holbein also illustrated other books, including Martin Luther's German translation of the Bible. In addition he painted pictures and portraits and, like his father, designed stained-glass windows. He also created designs for a series of 41 woodcuts called *The Dance of Death*.

In about 1525 the factional strife that accompanied the Reformation made Basel a difficult place for an artist to work. In 1526 Holbein, carrying a letter of introduction from Erasmus to the English statesman and author Sir Thomas More, set out for London. He met with a favorable reception in England and stayed there for two years. In 1528 he returned to Basel, where he painted portraits and murals for the town hall. In 1532 he left his wife and children there and traveled once again to London.

In England, where he became court painter to Henry VIII, Holbein was known chiefly as a painter of portraits. His services were much in demand. The more than 100 miniature and full-size portraits he completed at Henry's court provide a remarkable document of that colorful period. An old account of his services at court relates that he painted the portrait of the king, "life size, so well that everyone who looks is astonished, since it seems to live as if it moved its head and limbs." In spite of their richness of detail, Holbein's portraits provide remarkably little insight into the personality and character of the people he painted.

Holbein also found time to perform numerous services for Henry. He designed the king's state robes and made drawings that were the basis of all kinds of items used by the royal household, from buttons to bridles to book bindings. In 1539, when Henry was thinking of marrying Anne of Cleves, he sent Holbein to paint her portrait. In 1543 Holbein was in London working on another portrait of the king when he died, a victim of the plague.

WINSLOW HOMER

(b. 1836–d. 1910)

One of the greatest of American painters, Winslow Homer is best known for his watercolors and oil paintings of the sea. These paintings often have great dramatic effect because of the way they show man's powerlessness in the face of the unfeeling forces of nature.

The Gulf Stream by American painter Winslow Homer. De Agostini/Getty Images

Homer was born on Feb. 24, 1836, in Boston, Mass. When he was 6 his family moved to nearby Cambridge, where he became fond of outdoor life. His mother, an amateur artist, encouraged his interest in art, and at 19 he was apprenticed to a lithographer in Boston. He quickly developed skill in line drawing, and two years later he opened a studio.

In 1859 he moved to New York City, where he worked as an illustrator. His first big assignment was to sketch Abraham Lincoln's presidential inauguration for *Harper's Weekly*. During the Civil War Homer was an artist-correspondent. He also began exhibiting some of his paintings at the National Academy of Design. Homer turned some of his army-life sketches into oils. Encouraged by the reception they received, he gave up illustrating. His first paintings told a story, usually of some everyday occurrence. Art critics of the time were unimpressed. Today these story paintings, though generally considered to be inferior to his later work, serve as valuable records of 19th-century life. Homer's most familiar paintings include *Snap the Whip*, which dates from 1872, *Fog Warning* (1885), and *The Gulf Stream* (1899).

Homer spent 1881 and 1882 in Tynemouth on the coast of north-eastern England. When he returned to the United States, he settled in Prout's Neck on the coast of Maine. There he did some of his finest work. Aside from frequent trips—to the Adirondacks, Florida, and the Caribbean—he lived there for the rest of his life. Homer never married. He died in Prout's Neck on Sept. 29, 1910.

EDWARD HOPPER

(b. 1882–d. 1967)

The American painter Edward Hopper used bright colors to depict ordinary scenes from everyday life. His paintings were done in such a way as to create a somber, melancholy mood. Snapshot-like compositions such as *Nighthawks* (1942) used the eerie light of an all-night diner to isolate the customers and foster an inescapable sense of loneliness.

Hopper was born in Nyack, N.Y., on July 22, 1882. In 1899 he went to New York City to study at the New York School of Art. He was trained primarily as an illustrator, but between 1901 and 1906 he studied painting under Robert Henri, the realist painter and leader of the Ashcan School of realism. Three trips to Europe in the years 1906 to 1910 exposed Hopper to the experimentation going on in France, but the new ideas did not influence him. Apart from summers in New England, he lived in New York City.

Although he exhibited at the Armory Show of 1913 in New York City, Hopper devoted most of his time to advertising and illustrative etchings until 1924. He then took up painting full time.

Like other artists of the Ashcan School, Hopper depicted commonplace scenes from city life. But, unlike their loosely organized, vivacious paintings, his *House by the Railroad* (1925) and *Room in Brooklyn* (1932) show still, anonymous figures and stern geometric forms within snapshot-like compositions that create an inescapable sense of loneliness. His subjects included city streets, roadside lunch counters, Victorian homes, New England cottages, barren apartments, and theater interiors. All exhibit a pervasive calm with no hint of urban congestion. Among his works are *Early Sunday Morning* (1930) and *Second Story Sunlight* (1960).

Hopper's first one-man show was in 1920. Later in life he had major retrospective shows at the Museum of Modern Art and the Whitney Museum of American Art in New York City. He died in New York City on May 15, 1967.

JEAN-AUGUSTE-DOMINIQUE INGRES

(b. 1780–d. 1867)

In the mid-19th century, Jean-Auguste-Dominique Ingres was a leader of the neoclassical, as opposed to the Romantic, school of painting in France. He influenced considerably such later artists as Edgar Degas, Pierre-Auguste Renoir, and Pablo Picasso.

Jean-Auguste-Dominique Ingres was born on Aug. 29, 1780, in Montauban, France. His education began when he was 6 but was interrupted by the French Revolution. At age 11 he began studying at the Academy of Toulouse. From age 13 to 16 Ingres supported himself by playing violin in an opera orchestra. He continued to play the violin for pleasure for the rest of his life, but at 17 he was in Paris studying under the renowned Jacques-Louis David, the leading neoclassical painter of the time. For the next several years he worked successfully in Paris, winning various competitions and completing some of his most famous portraits.

From 1806 to 1824 Ingres was in Italy, first in Rome and then Florence, producing historical pictures, pencil portraits, and religious works. In 1829 he was named professor at the Paris École des Beaux-Arts. Except for a period in Italy as director of the French Academy in Rome from 1835 to 1841, he remained in Paris for the rest of his life.

During the late 1840s and 1850s Ingres painted an impressive number of superb portraits of men and women as well as his famous "Self-Portrait." He died on Jan. 14, 1867, bequeathing the enormous contents of his studio to his native city, Montauban. In addition to about 4,000 drawings and some well-known paintings, the bequest included his reference library, notebooks, wooden models for his classical structures, and his famous violin.

JASPER JOHNS

(b. 1930–)

U.S. artist Jasper Johns was one of the leading artists associated with the pop art movement. He took as his subject the most common and even bland of U.S. symbols—maps of the 48 continental states, the flag, numbers—and depicted these immediately identifiable symbols with meditative and intelligent scrutiny. Through his work, he attempted to make people see familiar objects in a new way.

Johns was born on May 15, 1930, in Augusta, Ga. He studied briefly at the University of South Carolina at Columbia in 1947–48 and then

Pop artist Jasper Johns next to Target, one of his mixed-media works. Ben Martin/ Time & Life Pictures/Getty Images

moved to New York City to pursue a career as an artist. In 1954 he became friends with fellow artist Robert Rauschenberg, and they greatly influenced each other's development as artists. That same year he began his series of paintings of U.S. flags, a subject which came to him in a dream. After years of struggling financially and creatively, Johns's first one-man show, held at the Leo Castelli Gallery in New York City in 1958, was a resounding success.

The paintings Johns went on to produce depict commonplace, two-dimensional subjects such as flags, targets, maps, numbers, and letters of the alphabet, all easily recognizable and painted in simple colors. He was able to elevate these objects to icons through his paint handling and a sensitive manipulation of surface texture, which he obtained by the encaustic technique, in which paint is mixed with hot liquid wax. In their intentional banality and rejection of emotional expression, these early works were a radical departure from the abstract expressionist styles that dominated the U.S. art scene at the time. Johns's depiction of everyday emblems and objects greatly influenced the pop art movement. He created numerous sculptures of mass-produced items including beer cans, flashlights, and lightbulbs. One of his best-known works is a cast sculpture of two Ballantine Ale cans, *Painted Bronze* (1960). The use of common subjects explored the meaning of art itself and the difference between life and art.

Beginning in 1961 Johns began to affix real objects, including brooms, brushes, and coat hangers, to the surface of his canvases. While continuing to paint numbers, flags, and labels through the early 1960s, he also began to incorporate more fluid brush strokes and rawer paint textures in such works as *Diver* (1962). During this time, lithographs became an important part of his work. Changing his style in the 1970s, Johns produced near-monochrome paintings composed of clusters of parallel lines that he called "crosshatchings." His subject motifs for these works often were taken from glimpses of patterns such as on flagstones or shadows on cars. Departing from his earlier emotionless and impersonal subjects, the paintings he did after about 1980 contain both figural elements and autobiographical references. Johns was awarded the Presidential Medal of Freedom in 2011.

LOIS MAILOU JONES

(b. 1905–d. 1998)

U.S. painter and educator Lois Mailou Jones was born in Boston, Mass., on Nov. 3, 1905. She studied at the Boston High School of Practical Arts, the Boston Museum School of Fine Arts, and the Designers Art School. She won fellowships for study in Paris and Italy in the late 1930s and received a bachelor's degree in art education from Howard University in 1945, graduating magna cum laude. She came to prominence as a textile designer and fashion illustrator. Later she painted in oil and in watercolors, with an emphasis on African American subjects. (Jones herself was African American, but she expressed hope that someday such distinctions would be unnecessary.) She became a professor at Howard University in 1930, where she taught painting as well as design until 1977. Jones divided her time between homes in Washington, D.C., Martha's Vineyard, and Haiti.

Jones won more than 50 awards, beginning in 1940 with a first prize from the National Museum for an oil painting and including the White House Outstanding Achievement in the Arts award presented to her by President Jimmy Carter in 1980. She also won several awards from the National Gallery in Washington, D.C., became a fellow of the Royal Society of Arts in London, and won a 1955 Diplôme et Décoration de l'Ordre National, Honneur et Mérite au Grade de Chevalier from the Government of Haiti.

Some of Jones's paintings include *Old Street in Montmartre, The Ascent of Ethiopia* (1932), *Jennie* (1943), *Homage to Senghor* (1976), and *Speracedes*. *Homage to Senghor* was presented to President Léopold Senghor of Senegal for his 70th birthday. Her work, which included paintings in impressionist, abstract, and African-influenced styles, was noted for strong color and design. Jones exhibited widely in group shows as well as alone. Her solo exhibition at the Boston Museum of Fine Arts was the first such exhibition by an African American artist. In 1988 she presented a gallery exhibition entitled Lois Mailou Jones: 58 Years of Watercolors 1930–1988. Her works were in many of the major

collections in museums, universities, and private collections, includ-
ing the Brooklyn Museum, the Hirshhorn Museum, the Metropolitan
Museum of Art, IBM Corporation, the Rosenwald Foundation, and the
Walker Art Center. Jones died on June 9, 1998, in Washington, D.C.

FRIDA KAHLO

(b. 1907–d. 1954)

Mexican painter Frida Kahlo created intense, brilliantly colored
self-portraits painted in a primitivistic style. She drew inspiration from her Mexican heritage and incorporated native and religious
symbols into her work. She twice married artist Diego Rivera, who both
encouraged and influenced her painting.

Magdalena Carmen Frida Kahlo y Calderón was born on July 6,
1907, in Coyoacán, Mexico. Except for getting basic artistic training in
her father's photography studio and taking two classes when she was
a student, she was self-taught as an artist. In 1925 she was involved in a
bus accident that so seriously injured her that she underwent some
three dozen operations. During her slow recovery from the trauma,
Kahlo began to paint. She showed her early efforts to Rivera, whom she
had met a few years earlier, and he encouraged her to continue to paint.
Nearly half of Kahlo's works are self-portraits, in which she explores
her identity as a woman, as a Mexican, and as an artist. Because of her
ongoing medical problems, the portraits frequently portray her in
physical agony.

After Kahlo married Rivera in 1929, she traveled with him for a few
years in the United States, where he had received commissions for several
murals. Her time in the United States strengthened her Mexican nation-
alism, and after returning to Mexico she continued to champion Mexican
national identity and culture. She was politically active as a Communist
and gave refuge to exiled Soviet leader Leon Trotsky in the late 1930s.
Kahlo and Rivera's relationship was intense, complex, and strained by
many infidelities. They separated in 1939 but remarried in 1941.

In 1938 Kahlo met André Breton, a leading surrealist, who cham-
pioned her work. Both Breton and Marcel Duchamp were influential

in arranging some of the exhibits of her work in the United States and Europe. Although Kahlo became identified as a surrealist, she disavowed that label. In 1943 she was appointed a professor of painting at La Esmeralda, the Education Ministry's School of Fine Arts. After suffering from poor health for years because of her accident, Kahlo died on July 13, 1954, in Coyoacán. *The Diary of Frida Kahlo,* covering the years of 1944–54, and *The Letters of Frida Kahlo* were both published in 1995. *Frida*, a movie about her life, was released in 2002, with Mexican actress Salma Hayek portraying Kahlo.

WASSILY KANDINSKY

(b. 1866–d. 1944)

Ranked among the artists whose work changed the history of art in the early years of the 20th century, the Russian abstract painter Wassily Kandinsky is generally regarded as one of the originators of abstract painting, or abstract expressionism. In both his painting and his theoretical writings he influenced modern styles. Spending many years of his life in Germany, Kandinsky became an instrumental force in the development of German expressionism.

Kandinsky was born in Moscow on Dec. 4, 1866. He studied law and political economy at the University of Moscow, but after a visit in 1895 to an exhibition of French impressionist paintings in Moscow, Kandinsky decided to become a painter. Moving to Munich, Germany, he worked under Anton Azbé and Franz von Stuck, studying impressionist color and art nouveau (an ornamental style of about 1890 to 1910). From the very beginning Kandinsky's own work showed an interest in fantasy.

Between 1900 and 1910 Kandinsky traveled widely, including visits to Paris that put him in contact with the art of Paul Gauguin, the neoimpressionists, and fauvism (a style with aggressive use of brilliant colors). He began developing his ideas concerning the power of pure color and nonrepresentational painting. In 1909 Kandinsky helped found the New Artists' Association in Munich.

Kandinsky painted his first abstract watercolor in 1910 and began formulating his important theoretical study, *Concerning the Spiritual in*

Art, which was published originally in German in 1912. In this work he examined the psychological effects of color and made comparisons between painting and music. Together with the German painter Franz Marc, Kandinsky became a leader in the influential Blaue Reiter (Blue Rider) movement, an expressionist group. He and Marc edited a Blue Rider almanac in which they reproduced art from all ages.

Marc and Kandinsky organized avant-garde international exhibitions in Munich and elsewhere—exhibitions that proved to be major events in the development of German expressionism. With the outbreak of World War I, Kandinsky left Germany to return to Russia, where he taught and organized numerous artistic activities. He went back to Germany in 1921 and became one of the principal teachers at the Bauhaus school in Weimar, remaining with the school until it was closed by the Nazi regime in 1933. Kandinsky then moved to a Parisian suburb, where he stayed until his death on Dec. 13, 1944.

A significant change took place in Kandinsky's work during the 1920s. From the romantic superabundance of his earlier abstract expressionism, his style evolved into geometric forms—points, bundles of lines, circles, and triangles. During the last decade of his life, Kandinsky blended the free, intuitive image of his earlier years with the geometric forms of his Bauhaus period.

ANISH KAPOOR

(b. 1954–)

Indian-born British sculptor Anish Kapoor is known for his use of abstract biomorphic (abstract designs resembling living life forms) forms and his penchant for rich colors and polished surfaces. He was also the first living artist to be given a solo show at the Royal Academy of Arts in London.

Kapoor was born on March 12, 1954 in Bombay (now Mumbai) in India to parents of Punjabi and Iraqi-Jewish heritage. He moved to London to study at the Hornsey College of Art (1973–77) and the Chelsea School of Art (1977–78). A return visit to India in 1979 sparked off new perspectives on the land of his birth. These were reflected through his

Anish Kapoor, posing with one of his pieces prior to the opening of an exhibit of his works in Berlin, Germany, in 2013. Adam Berry/Getty Images

use of saturated or drenched coloring and striking architectural forms in bodies of work such as *1000 Names*. Created between 1979 and 1980, this series consisted of arrangements of abstract geometric forms coated with loose powdered pigments that spilled beyond the object itself and onto the floor or wall.

During the 1980s and '90s Kapoor was increasingly recognized for his biomorphic sculptures and installations, made with materials as varied as stone, aluminum, and resin, which appeared to challenge gravity, depth, and perception. In 1990 he represented Great Britain at the Venice Biennale with his installation *Void Field*, a grid of rough sandstone blocks, each with a mysterious black hole penetrating its top surface. The following year he was honored with the Turner Prize, a prestigious award for contemporary art. Kapoor continued to explore

the idea of the void during the remainder of the decade, creating series of works that built in constructions that withdrew into walls, disappeared into floors, or dramatically changed depth with a simple change in perspective.

In the early 21st century Kapoor's interest in addressing site and architecture led him to create projects that were increasingly ambitious in scale and construction. For his 2002 installation *Marsyas* at the Tate Modern gallery in London, Kapoor created a trumpet-like form by erecting three massive steel rings joined by a 550-foot (155-meter) span of fleshy red plastic membrane that stretched the length of the museum's Turbine Hall. In 2004 Kapoor unveiled *Cloud Gate* in Chicago's Millennium Park; the 110-ton oval archway of highly polished stainless steel—nicknamed "The Bean"—was his first permanent site-specific installation in the United States. For just over a month in 2006, Kapoor's *Sky Mirror*, a concave stainless-steel mirror 35 feet (11 metres) in diameter, was installed in New York City's Rockefeller Center. Both *Cloud Gate* and *Sky Mirror* reflected and transformed their surroundings and demonstrated Kapoor's ongoing investigation of material, form, and space.

Kapoor's later works include *ArcelorMittal Orbit* (completed 2011), a 377-foot (115-meter) tower surrounded by a looping lattice of red tubular steel. The structure, commissioned by the city of London for the 2012 Olympic Games, stood in London's Olympic Park, and an observation deck at the top of the tower opened to the public in conjunction with the sporting event.

Kapoor was made Commander of the Order of the British Empire (CBE) in 2003, and he was named a knight bachelor in 2013. He received the Japan Art Association's Praemium Imperiale prize for sculpture in 2011.

PAUL KLEE

(b. 1879–d. 1940)

One of the most inventive and admired painters to emerge from the 20th-century rebellion against representational, or realistic, art was Paul Klee. Fantasy and striking use of color characterize his work.

Paul Klee was born on Dec. 18, 1879, near Bern, Switzerland. His parents were musicians, and he became an accomplished violinist. After attending school in Bern, he went to Munich, where he studied art from 1898 to 1901. He returned to Bern but was soon off for a trip to Italy. The Renaissance masters were of particular interest to him, as were the impressionists on his journeys to Paris in 1905 and 1912. Klee taught at the Weimar Bauhaus from 1921 to 1924 and at the Dessau Bauhaus from 1926 to 1931. When the Nazis came to power in 1933, they condemned his work. Klee then returned to Switzerland.

Klee was one of the Blaue Reiter (Blue Rider) artists, who led Germany's experiments in nonobjective art before World War I. His early works were chiefly drawings and etchings. After a trip in 1914 to Tunisia, where he was deeply impressed by the colors he saw, he turned to painting. Later Klee contributed to the art theory of the Bauhaus school, which influenced industrial design, architecture, and painting. He developed pictorial themes in the way a composer develops musical themes. His output ranges from highly realistic portraiture to the abstractionism of such paintings as *Villa R* and *Fugue in Red*. Later works—*Fear* and *Death and Fire*, for example—reflect his concern with the approach of his death and of war. He died at Muralto, near Locarno, on June 29, 1940.

GUSTAV KLIMT

(b. 1862–d. 1918)

As a founder of the school of art known as the Vienna Secession, Austrian painter Gustav Klimt revolted against academic art in favor of a highly decorative style similar to art nouveau. He is best known for his murals and portraits of women.

Klimt was born on July 14, 1862, in Vienna. After studying at the Vienna School of Decorative Arts, he and his brother Ernst in 1883 opened an independent studio specializing in the execution of mural paintings. His early work was typical of late 19th-century academic painting, as can be seen in his murals for the Vienna Burgtheater (1888) and on the staircase of the Kunsthistorisches Museum.

After the death of his brother in 1892, Klimt stopped painting for a time. In 1897 Klimt's mature style emerged, and he cofounded the Vienna Secession, which also included German architects Josef Hoffmann, and Joseph Olbrich. A later group was formed, also led by Klimt, centering on an exhibition known as the Kunstschau, from which emerged some of the most illustrious modern Austrian painters, including Oskar Kokoschka, Alfred Kubin, and Egon Schiele.

The three allegorical murals Klimt painted for the ceiling of the University of Vienna auditorium were greatly criticized. The erotic symbolism and pessimism of these works created such a scandal that the murals were rejected. His later murals, the *Beethoven Frieze* (1902) and the murals (1909–11) in the dining room of the Stoclet House in Brussels, are characterized by precisely linear drawing and the bold and arbitrary use of flat, decorative patterns of color and gold leaf. Klimt's most successful works include *The Kiss* (1908) and a series of portraits he did of fashionable Viennese matrons, such as *Frau Fritza Riedler* (1906) and *Frau Adele Bloch-Bauer* (1907). In these works he treats the human figure without shadow and heightens the skin by surrounding it with areas of flat, highly ornamental, and brilliantly composed areas of decoration. Klimt died on Feb. 6, 1918, in Vienna.

WILLEM DE KOONING

(b. 1904–d. 1997)

A major abstract expressionist painter, Willem de Kooning is best known for his controversial paintings of women. He was considered by some to be the foremost American artist of the 1950s.

De Kooning was born on April 24, 1904, in Rotterdam, the Netherlands. In 1916 he was apprenticed to a firm of commercial artists and began attending evening classes at an art academy. He went to New York City in 1926 and worked as a freelance commercial artist. From 1935 to 1937 he worked for the Works Progress Administration (WPA) Federal Art Project, and in 1939 he designed a mural for the Hall of Pharmacy at the New York World's Fair. He taught art at Black

Willem de Kooning, mixing paint in his Long Island (New York) studio in the 1960s.
Ben Van Meerondonk/Archive Photos/Getty Images

Mountain College in North Carolina in 1948 and at Yale University from 1950 to 1951.

De Kooning started painting in an abstract style in about 1934 and was considered a major avant-garde painter by the mid-1940s. His paintings of the 1930s and 1940s centered on men, women, and abstractions. In 1946, he turned to black and white household enamels to paint a series of large abstractions. His works became progressively more violent, causing controversy at their gallery showing in 1953 because of de Kooning's blatant figurative technique and imagery used to create harsh, grossly sexual women. By the late 1950s he painted in a more symbolic style, absorbing female figures into landscape backgrounds. Later he began devoting much time to sculpting in clay and began painting in a cleaner style. De Kooning developed Alzheimer's disease and died in his studio on Long Island on March 19, 1997.

JEFF KOONS

(b. 1955–)

J eff Koons was one of a number of American artists to emerge in the 1980s with an aesthetic devoted to the decade's pervasive consumer culture. Koons managed to shock the art world with one daring work after another, from displaying commercial vacuum cleaners and basketballs as his own art to making porcelain reproductions of kitsch objects (objects seen as having little style and indicating the lack of taste of the buyer) to showing homemade pornography.

Koons was born on Jan. 21, 1955, in York, Pa. After studying at the School of the Art Institute in Chicago and working with the Chicago artist Ed Paschke, Koons graduated from the Maryland Institute of Art (B.F.A., 1976) and then moved to New York City, where he sold memberships at the Museum of Modern Art. He later worked as a commodities broker on Wall Street while making art during off-hours. In the early 1980s he began making art full-time.

In his early years Koons characteristically worked in series. To name only a few, a series called *The New* (1980–83) included commercial vacuum cleaners and floor polishers in glass cabinets; his *Equilibrium* series (1985) consisted of cast bronze flotation devices and basketballs suspended in fluid; and his *Made in Heaven* series (1990–91) was a group of erotic paintings and sculptures of Koons and his former wife, Italian porn star Cicciolina (Ilona Staller). Koons was an early pioneer of appropriation, which called for reproducing ordinary and boring commercial images and objects with only slight modifications in scale or material.

In the first decade of the 21st century, he was best known for his fabricated objects from commercial sources—primarily inflatable pool toys and balloon animals—in highly polished and colored stainless steel, and for his paintings that layer and set side by side various commercial and popular motifs. Koons was part of the post-pop generation (which also included Cindy Sherman and Richard Prince), who continued to pursue the '60s pop movement's fascination with popular culture and advertising, as well as the social codes reinforced by the dominant media. In the manner of Andy Warhol, Koons established a large studio/factory in New York City's Chelsea neighborhood, where dozens of employees produce the work that he conceives.

LEE KRASNER

(b. 1908–d. 1984)

Lee Krasner was an American painter recognized for her unique contribution to abstract expressionism.

Lee Krasner was born Lenore Krassner on October 27, 1908, in Brooklyn, New York. Krasner was the sixth of seven children of Jewish emigrants from Odessa, Russia (now Ukraine). When she was 13 she decided to become an artist and chose to study at Washington Irving High School, the only public high school in New York City at that time that offered women professional art training. After graduation she studied first at the Women's Art School of Cooper Union and then, in her early 20s, at the National Academy of Design, both in New York.

The American government's New Deal Federal Art Project enabled Krasner to work full-time as an artist from 1934 to 1943. During that time she studied with the hugely influential German painter Hans Hofmann, who exposed her to Pablo Picasso's use of form in synthetic cubism as well as Henri Matisse's use of color and outline. Blending these European influences, Krasner developed her own style of geometric abstraction, which she grounded in floral motifs and rhythmic gesture. In 1940 she began exhibiting her work with that of other American abstract artists. Her forceful personality and passion for painting soon brought her to the center of the New York art world, a largely male arena that was in the midst of intense ideological agitation.

In 1942 Krasner met the painter Jackson Pollock, whose work was being exhibited along with hers in a New York gallery. She was struck by the power of his work, and the two artists became friends. After their 1945 marriage the couple moved to a farm in East Hampton, New York. Each artist influenced the other to some extent. In 1946 she began her *Little Image* paintings, a tightly focused series of works in which her use of dots and drips of paint were inspired by Pollock's "drip paintings" of the period. In these and her collages of the early 1950s, Krasner often worked on a small scale, which separated her work from that of the other abstract expressionists. Her work was also unique in terms of her commitment (in varying degrees) to maintaining some figuration— usually patterns from nature, sometimes calligraphic elements like Hebrew letters—and an intellectual sense of control, in contrast to the less-controlled automatism being practiced by her contemporaries. In the years after Pollock's death in 1956, however, she created a series of enormous paintings filled with thick, expressive strokes of umbre paint that abandoned figuration and instead presented raw energy, perhaps in an attempt to express her overwhelming sense of grief. In the 1960s and '70s, Krasner continued her trademark explorations of color and graceful, rhythmic form in paintings and collages, using large-scale abstraction but also hard-edged figurative elements and a certain amount of intellectual control.

For years after Pollock's death, Krasner's reputation was eclipsed by his, partly because of her tireless advocacy of his work during his life and after his death. This perception changed when a 1981 show in New York, "Krasner/Pollock: A Working Relationship," helped demonstrate that she was both his artistic partner and a significant artist in her own right. A major retrospective of her work held at the Museum of Fine Arts in Houston, Texas, and the Museum of Modern Art in New York in 1983 further solidified her reputation. Krasner died July 19, 1984, in New York City. Her work is included in the collections of the world's major museums, and a major touring retrospective ended January 2001 at the Brooklyn Museum of Art.

DOROTHEA LANGE

(b. 1895–d. 1965)

The stark photographs of the victims of the Great Depression of the 1930s that were made by Dorothea Lange were a major influence on succeeding documentary and journalistic photographers. She has been called the greatest documentary photographer of the United States.

Dorothea Lange was born in Hoboken, N.J., on May 26, 1895. She first studied photography under Clarence White, a member of a well-known group of photographers called the Photo-Secession. At the age of 20 Lange decided to travel around the world, earning money as she went by selling her photographs. Her money ran out in San Francisco, where she settled and opened a portrait studio in 1916.

During the depression Lange photographed the homeless men who wandered the streets. Such pictures as *White Angel Breadline*, shot in 1932, showed the hopelessness of these men and received immediate recognition from the renowned photographers of Group f/64. This led to Lange's being hired by the federal Resettlement Administration (later called the Farm Security Administration) to bring the conditions of the poor to public attention. Her photographs of California's migrant workers, captioned with the subjects' own words, were so effective that the state established camps for the migrants.

In 1939 Lange published a collection of her photographs called *An American Exodus: A Record of Human Erosion*. Two years later she received a Guggenheim Fellowship, which she gave up in order to record with her camera the mass evacuation of Japanese-Americans in California to detention camps after the bombing of Pearl Harbor. Following World War II, Lange did a number of photo essays for *Life* magazine. On Oct. 11, 1965, she died in San Francisco after a long illness.

ANNIE LEIBOVITZ

(b. 1949–)

Annie Leibovitz is an American photographer renowned for her dramatic, quirky, and iconic portraits of a great variety of celebrities. Her signature style is crisp and well lighted.

Annie Leibovitz was born Anna-Lou Leibovitz on October 2, 1949, in Westbury, Conn. Her father had a military career, and her mother was a dancer. The family was living in the Philippines in 1967 when Leibovitz enrolled in the San Francisco Art Institute (B.F.A., 1971), intending to become a painter. After taking a night class in photography, she quickly became engrossed in that medium. In 1970, while still a student,

Popular photographer Annie Leibovitz (right) shows actor Russell Brand images of him she took during a 2011 photo shoot in California. Getty Images

she was given her first commercial assignment for *Rolling Stone* magazine: to photograph John Lennon. Three years later Leibovitz became the publication's chief photographer, creating a unique presentation of the major personalities of contemporary rock music. In 1975 she documented the Rolling Stones' six-month North American concert tour, during which she shot several widely reproduced photographs of guitarist Keith Richards and lead singer Mick Jagger. Perhaps her most famous work from this period is a portrait of Lennon and Yoko Ono that was published on the cover of *Rolling Stone* in January 1981. In the picture, shot mere hours before Lennon's assassination, the singer-songwriter is nude and wrapped in a fetus like position around his fully clothed wife.

In 1983 Leibovitz produced a 60-print show that toured Europe and the United States. The accompanying book, *Annie Leibovitz: Photographs*, was a best seller. That same year she joined the staff of *Vanity Fair*, which broadened her pool of subjects to include film stars, athletes, and political figures. For her portraits, Leibovitz—who viewed her photographic sessions as collaborations—typically spent days observing her subjects' daily lives and worked to make her portraits of them unique and witty, each a technically exquisite distillation. Her commercial images were dramatic and staged rather than casual.

She received the American Society of Magazine Photographers award for photographer of the year in 1983. She began to work as an advertising photographer in 1986, gaining such clients as Honda, American Express, and the Gap. The American Express ad campaign that used her photos won a Clio Award, recognizing advertising excellence worldwide, in 1987. She later was involved in the California Milk Processor Board (the "Got Milk?" campaign). In 2011 she photographed seven top female athletes for the sportswear company Nike's "Make Yourself" campaign. Her style throughout these projects was characterized by carefully staged settings, superb lighting, and her trademark use of vivid color.

In 1991 Leibovitz had her first museum exhibition; she became the first woman and second living photographer to show at the National Portrait Gallery in Washington, D.C. A companion book, *Photographs: Annie Leibovitz 1970-1990*, was published in 1991. She also earned much praise for her portraits of American Olympians taken for an exhibit at the 1996 Summer Games in Atlanta, Georgia, which were later published in the book *Olympic Portraits* (1996). In 1999 she published a collection of photographs titled *Women*, with an essay by intellectual and writer Susan Sontag, who was her lover.

In 2000 Leibovitz was among the first group of Americans to be designated a Library of Congress Living Legend. Among the later publications of her work were *American Music* (2003), *A Photographer's Life: 1990–2005* (2006), and *Annie Leibovitz at Work* (2008). Leibovitz's perfectionism in her work (budgets were exploded, and no expense was spared) and her celebrity-touched lifestyle had a role in producing a debt of $24 million, for which she was sued in 2009. The suit against her was settled. Later that year, her official portrait of the first family—Pres. Barack Obama, his wife, Michelle, and his daughters, Sasha and Malia—was released to the public. The photographer's achievements were also celebrated in *Annie Leibovitz: Life Through a Lens* (2009), a documentary film. During her financial difficulties, Leibovitz began working on a personal project, photographing places and objects that were meaningful to her, and the images were collected in the book *Pilgrimage* (2011).

LEONARDO DA VINCI

(b. 1452–d. 1519)

The term "Renaissance man" was coined to describe the genius of Leonardo da Vinci. He was a man of so many accomplishments in so many areas of human endeavor that his like has rarely been seen in human history. Casual patrons of the arts know him as the painter of *La Gioconda*, more commonly called the *Mona Lisa*, and of the exquisite *Last Supper*, painted on the wall of the dining hall in the monastery of Santa Maria delle Grazie in Milan, Italy.

More than 300 years before flying machines were perfected, Leonardo devised plans for prototypes of an airplane and a helicopter. His extensive studies of human anatomy were portrayed in anatomical drawings, which were among the most significant achievements of Renaissance science. His remarkable illustrations of the human body elevated drawing into a means of scientific investigation and exposition and provided the basic principles for modern scientific illustration.

79

LIFE OF LEONARDO

The life of Leonardo da Vinci can be divided into five distinct periods: his childhood and youth in Florence, Italy; his first stay in Milan from 1482 to 1499; the second Florentine period from 1500 to 1506; his second stay in Milan from 1506 to 1513; and his last six years from 1513 to 1519, which were divided equally between Rome and Amboise, France, where he worked for King Francis I.

CHILDHOOD AND YOUTH

Leonardo was born in 1452 on his father's family estate at Vinci, near Florence, where he was also raised and educated. When he was 15 his father apprenticed him to the artist Andrea del Verrocchio in Florence. Under Verrocchio he studied painting, sculpture, and the mechanical arts. In the nearby workshop of the artist Antonio Pollaiuolo he began his interest in anatomy. Leonardo was accepted into the painters' guild at Florence in 1472 and remained in the city for the next ten years.

Even in this early period of his life, Leonardo's mastery of his art was evident, especially in two unfinished paintings: *St. Jerome* and *The Adoration of the Magi*. There were also a number of pen and pencil drawings that gave evidence of his great skill in sketching. Many of these drawings were of a technical nature—pumps, military weaponry, and other mechanical apparatus.

FIRST SERVICE IN MILAN

In 1482 Leonardo was hired by the duke of Milan, Ludovico Sforza, to be artist and engineer in residence. In this capacity he was constantly kept busy as a painter and sculptor, though many of his paintings and all of his sculptures remained unfinished.

Leonardo was also frequently consulted by workmen in the fields of architecture, fortifications, and weaponry; and he served as a hydraulic and mechanical engineer. It was while he was in Milan that the full versatility of his genius began to unfold, and the full range of his interests in the world of mankind and nature in general became evident. Through his remarkable ability to understand what he saw, he determined to compose a unified theory of the world and to illustrate it in a series of voluminous notebooks. Unfortunately his relentless pursuit of scientific knowledge forced him to leave unfinished many of his planned artistic creations. Today they are known primarily from drawings in the notebooks.

In his 17 years in Milan, Leonardo completed only six paintings: two portraits, the *Last Supper*, two versions of *The Virgin of the Rocks*, and a decorative ceiling painting in the Castello Sforzesco. Other commissioned paintings were either not done or have disappeared.

RETURN TO FLORENCE

Ludovico Sforza was driven from power by a French army in 1499. At the end of the year, or early in 1500, Leonardo returned to his home city after visits to Mantua and Venice. After his long absence, he was received as an honored and renowned artist.

In Florence, as in Milan, he was commissioned to do a number of paintings. The most notable work to survive from this period was the *Mona Lisa*. His largest commission, a huge mural entitled *Battle of Anghiari* for the Palazzo Vecchio, Florence's city hall, remained unfinished.

For ten months during 1502, Leonardo served as military adviser and engineer under Cesare Borgia in the latter's campaign to subdue the Papal States. He traveled through Borgia's territories, surveyed them, and made sketches of city plans and topographical maps that laid the groundwork for the field of modern cartography.

Back in Florence in 1503, Leonardo worked on the complicated engineering project of diverting the Arno River around Pisa in order to deprive the city of its access to the sea. The plan did not work, but it became the basis of a later project (never realized) to build a canal from Florence to the sea. He also busied himself with dissections of corpses at the hospital of Santa Maria Nuova, made observations on the flight of birds, and continued studies of the properties of water and its currents.

Leonardo da Vinci's iconic masterpiece, *Mona Lisa*, on display at the Louvre Museum in Paris. Eric Vandeville/Gamma-Rapho/Getty Images

SECOND STAY IN MILAN

In May 1506 Charles d'Amboise, governor of Milan for the king of France, invited Leonardo to return to that city. His work in painting and sculpture over the next seven years remained mostly in the planning stage, but his scientific work flourished. He continued his notebooks with observations and drawings of human anatomy, optics, mechanics, and botanical studies.

LAST YEARS

During the years 1513 to 1516, Leonardo was in Rome at the invitation of Cardinal Giuliano de' Medici, brother of Pope Leo X. Some of the greatest artists of the time were at work in Rome for the church. Leonardo, on the other hand, was not kept busy. He executed a map of the Pontine Marshes near Rome, suggesting that perhaps he was involved in a planned reclamation project. He also did some sketches for a Medici residence in Florence that was never built. Otherwise he was lonely and unoccupied. Thus in 1516, at the age of 65, he accepted an invitation from Francis I, king of France, to leave Italy and work for him.

Leonardo spent the last three years of his life in the palace of Cloux, near the king's residence at Amboise, near Tours. He was given the title of "first painter, architect, and mechanic of the King" and given freedom of action in what he wanted to do. He virtually abandoned painting to concentrate on his scientific studies. He finished the final drafts of his treatise on painting and worked on the study of anatomy. He also did a variety of sketches, including *Visions of the End of the World*, which testified to his undiminished ability as an artist.

For the king he drew plans for a palace and garden at Romorantin and made sketches for court festivals. Otherwise the king left him alone and treated him as an honored guest.

On May 2, 1519, Leonardo died at Cloux and was buried in the palace church. During the French Revolution the church, along with many other national monuments, was devastated and eventually torn down. The whereabouts of Leonardo's remains is no longer known.

LEONARDO'S LEGACY

Only 17 of the paintings that have survived can definitely be attributed to Leonardo, and not all of them are finished. Yet he is deservedly considered one of the greatest painters of all time. He excelled in inventiveness, technique, drawing ability, use of light, shadow, and color.

No sculpture survives that can be definitely attributed to Leonardo, but from the numerous sketches for unfinished projects it is known that he brought to sculpture the same ingenuity and inventiveness that he gave to painting. Two of his unfinished works were statues of men on horses—one a monumental figure in bronze to be erected in honor of Francesco Sforza, founder of the Sforza dynasty. He spent 12 years planning this statue, only to have the metal used for making cannon instead. But many sketches remain, and they give adequate evidence of Leonardo's concept of sculpture. The anatomical exactness of the horse, the proportions, and the feeling of movement in the sketches profoundly influenced the design of equestrian statues in the 17th century.

The greatest literary legacy any painter has ever bequeathed to the world is contained in the voluminous notebooks of Leonardo. His writing program began during the first stay in Milan, specifically between 1490 and 1495, when his strong inclination toward scientific studies showed itself.

Leonardo's notebooks are distinctive for two reasons: the relation of illustration to text and his use of "mirror writing." In the normal illustrated book, pictures amplify and clarify the text, but it is the text that contains the basic information. Although his language was clear and expressive, Leonardo always gave precedence to illustration over the written word. The drawings, therefore, do not illustrate the text, but the text serves to explain the pictures.

Mirror writing, as the term implies, means putting words down on paper in such a way that they can be read normally only when the page is held up to a mirror. Leonardo was quite adept at this, probably partly because he was left-handed. The reason for using mirror writing is uncertain because he did not intend to keep his notebooks a secret.

Exactly how many notebooks Leonardo composed is not known. In all, 31 have been preserved. In addition to these, there are other bundles of documents, or codexes, by Leonardo that have found their way into various European museums.

One of the most exciting finds of the 20th century was the discovery early in 1967 of 700 lost pages of manuscripts and drawings in the Spanish National Library in Madrid. These pages of Leonardo's work, bound in two volumes, had been missing for about 200 years. They contain, among other things, sketches of the large equestrian statue for the tomb of Francesco Sforza and drawings of complex gears, hydraulic machines, and other devices.

ROY LICHTENSTEIN

(b. 1923–d. 1997)

A painter who was a pioneer in the so-called pop art movement, Roy Lichtenstein took his subject matter from the phenomena of mass culture. The first one-man show of his cartoon paintings in New York City in 1962 was considered to be a sensation.

Roy Lichtenstein was born in New York City on Oct. 27, 1923. He received a master of fine arts degree from Ohio State University, where he taught from 1946 to 1951. He also taught at New York State University

College, in Oswego, and at Douglass College of Rutgers University, in New Brunswick, N.J.

In 1951, at the beginning of his career, Lichtenstein painted cowboys and Indians in modern art styles. His interest in the comic-strip cartoon as an art theme probably began in 1960 with a painting he made for his children of the Walt Disney character Mickey Mouse. As his technique developed, the comic-strip characters were greatly enlarged, including the tiny, barely noticeable dots that make up the image in most pictures printed in newspapers and comic books. Lichtenstein simulated and enlarged these dots by using a metal screen as a stencil. Bright colors and black outlines added to this technique, which resulted in paintings that were a combination of abstract and commercial art.

Lichtenstein also drew subjects from romance magazines, with their words in typical comic-strip balloons, and created landscapes using the comic-strip technique. His sculptures of the late 1960s derived from the glass-and-chrome styles of the 1930s era. Lichtenstein died in New York City on Sept. 29, 1997.

RENÉ MAGRITTE

(b. 1898–d. 1967)

The paintings of Belgian artist René Magritte are full of strange flights of fancy. His works repeatedly include certain symbols—a female torso, a middle-class man wearing a bowler hat, a castle, a rock, a window, and others. The illogical arrangements of his mysterious images blend horror, peril, comedy, and wonder. He was one of the most prominent surrealist painters, and he also influenced future generations of painters, especially pop artists and conceptual artists.

René-François-Ghislain Magritte was born on November 21, 1898, in Lessines, Belgium. He studied at the Brussels Academy of Fine Arts from 1916 to 1918. Afterward he became a designer for a wallpaper factory and later made sketches for advertisements. He experimented with several artistic styles such as cubism and futurism before 1922, when he saw a reproduction of Giorgio de Chirico's dreamlike painting *The*

Song of Love (1914). De Chirico's work places odd elements including a classical bust and a rubber glove side by side. It had a great influence on Magritte's mature style. For the next few years he was active in the Belgian surrealist movement. With the support of a Brussels art gallery, he became a full-time painter in 1926.

Magritte's first solo show was held in 1927, but it was not well received by the art critics of his day. That same year he and his wife moved to a suburb of Paris. There he met and befriended several of the Paris surrealists, including poets André Breton and Paul Éluard. He also became familiar with the collages of Max Ernst. In 1930 Magritte returned to Brussels, where he remained for the rest of his life. During the 1940s he experimented with a variety of styles, but the paintings he produced were not successful by most accounts. He eventually abandoned the experiments. For the rest of his life he continued to produce his enigmatic and illogical images in a readily identifiable style. In his last year he supervised the construction of eight bronze sculptures derived from images in his paintings. Magritte died on Aug. 15, 1967, in Brussels.

The sea and wide skies, which were enthusiasms of his childhood, figure strongly in his paintings. In *Threatening Weather* (1928) the clouds have the shapes of a torso, a tuba, and a chair. A huge stone topped by a small castle floats above the sea in *The Castle of the Pyrenees* (1959). Other typical fancies in his paintings were a fish with human legs, a man with a birdcage for a torso, and a gentleman leaning over a wall beside his pet lion. Dislocations of space, time, and scale were common elements. In *Time Transfixed* (1939), for example, a steaming locomotive is suspended from the center of a mantelpiece in a middle-class sitting room, looking as if it had just emerged from a tunnel.

ÉDOUARD MANET

(b. 1832–d. 1883)

The French painter whose work inspired the impressionists was Édouard Manet. Manet also introduced the technique of lighting faces or figures from the front, almost eliminating shadows. This method, called *peinture claire*, is now considered one of the basic technical

contributions of 19th-century art. Manet, who preferred to paint from nature, chose to picture things in the present and as he saw them. In addition to a representation of the object painted, Manet perceived his work as an arrangement of paint areas on a canvas.

Édouard Manet was born in Paris on Jan. 23, 1832. When he finished his studies at the Collège Rollin in 1848, he was determined to become an artist. His father, Auguste Manet, who worked at the Ministry of Justice, wanted him to study law. Rather than give in to his father, Édouard shipped out to Brazil as a cadet navigator. He returned in 1849, still intent on becoming an artist. His father relented, and at 18 Édouard began work under Thomas Couture, a prominent academic artist. After spending six years with Couture, Manet toured the galleries and museums of Europe, copying the old masters.

Two pictures that he painted in 1863—*Lunch on the Grass* and *Olympia*, which was first exhibited in 1865—made him a center of controversy in the French art world. In both paintings Manet used nude figures in modern settings and employed techniques that met with the disapproval of the French Academy. His break with tradition, however, won him the admiration of certain young artists. He became the leader of the group from which impressionism emerged.

Throughout his career Manet was primarily a painter of contemporary life. Typical of Manet's subjects was his last large canvas, *A Bar at the Folies-Bergère*. Although Manet never exhibited with the impressionists, he used their short brush strokes and bright colors in his later paintings. He died in Paris on April 30, 1883.

HENRI MATISSE

(b. 1869–d. 1954)

Widely regarded as the greatest French painter of the 20th century, Henri Matisse also excelled at sculpture, illustration, graphics, and scenic design. His final masterpiece, completed when he was more than 80 years old, was the complete decoration—including windows, furniture, vestments, and murals—for the Dominican Chapel of the Rosary in Vence, near Nice in southern France.

Henri Matisse was born in northern France, in Le Cateau, on Dec. 31, 1869. The son of a local grain merchant, Henri showed no early interest in art. Instead, after five years in a secondary school in Saint-Quentin, he went to Paris in 1887 to study law. In 1890, while recuperating from an attack of appendicitis, Matisse passed the time by trying his hand at painting with a set of oil paints that his mother had given him. "Henceforth," he wrote, "I did not lead my life. It led me."

Henri Matisse, sitting in front of glass panels he designed for his home in Nice, France. Gjon Mili//Time & Life Pictures/Getty Images

As a full-time art student in Paris, beginning in 1891, Matisse studied briefly with the popular painter and teacher Adolphe Bouguereau. He soon left Bouguereau, however, and began working under Gustave Moreau, who had Georges Rouault as one of his other students. Matisse showed skill as a copyist, and his early works, which won some recognition, were conventional still lifes and interiors—copies of Louvre masterpieces. Soon, however, he discovered the paintings of Pissarro, Cézanne, Monet, Gauguin, and other revolutionary artists of the day, and the easy life of a copyist lost its appeal for him.

Matisse began to experiment with impressionism and, later, with pointillism. He developed a radical new approach to color, using it in a structural rather than a descriptive way. His paintings, with their bold areas of flat, pure color, outraged the French art critics. At the 1905 Salon d'Automne, he exhibited *Woman with the Hat*, a portrait of his wife. At this show Matisse, Rouault, and their colleagues were given the nickname *les fauves* (French for "wild beasts") because their work was considered barbaric.

Despite public rejection in France, Matisse soon found appreciative buyers among a large circle of foreign patrons, including the influential American writer and art collector Gertrude Stein. In the next years he completed a number of paintings that are now acknowledged to be masterpieces of 20th-century art. The sensational 1913 Armory Show in New York City, which introduced Europe's modern art to the United States, included 13 of his paintings.

After his association with fauvism, which ended about 1907, Matisse never again belonged to any identifiable school or movement. He believed that an artist should not allow himself to become a prisoner of his style or reputation. His own works display tremendous versatility, ranging in style from austere and geometric to lush and decorative. After a visit to Morocco he began to use rich colors and exotic patterns. Other trips abroad added new images to his visual vocabulary.

Matisse married in 1898. He established his family in one of the suburbs of Paris and divided his time between the family home, his studio in Paris, and another studio on the French Riviera. In 1941, when he was in his 70s, an operation left him a semi-invalid. After that Matisse settled permanently on the Riviera. He continued working, however, producing such remarkable paintings as *Egyptian Curtain* and *Large Interior in Red* when he was in his late 70s and 80s. He died in Nice on Nov. 3, 1954.

Although he did not begin his artistic career until the age of 20, Matisse's output during the next 60 years was huge. In addition to hundreds of paintings, his works include many sculptures; graphics, both lithographs and etchings; and designs for tapestries. He prepared illustrations for *Poésies de Stéphane Mallarmé* (1932) and other books. He also designed the stage settings for several of Sergey Diaghilev's ballets.

In the last years of his life, Matisse created a series of works using shapes he cut from brightly colored paper. He also completed his designs for the small chapel at Vence, a picturesque little town where he had owned a villa from 1943 to 1948. He began the project by designing stained glass windows, went on to do murals and ended up by designing nearly everything inside and outside, including vestments and liturgical objects. The chapel is today one of the main tourist attractions near the Riviera.

MICHELANGELO

(b. 1475–d. 1564)

Sculptor, painter, architect, and poet Michelangelo was the greatest artist in a time of greatness. He lived during the Italian Renaissance, a period known for its creative activity. In art, the age's great achievement, Michelangelo led all others. He had a remarkable ability to concentrate his thoughts and energy on the task in hand. Often while working he would eat only a little bread, would sleep on the floor or on a cot beside his unfinished painting or statue, and would continue to wear the same clothes until his work was finished.

BEGINNINGS IN ART

Michelangelo di Lodovico Buonarroti Simoni was born on March 6, 1475. His birthplace, Caprese, Italy, was a tiny village that belonged to the nearby city-state of Florence. His father was the mayor of the village. The boy was the second of five brothers. He went to school in Florence, but his mind was on art, not on his studies. Even as a young child he was fascinated by painters and sculptors at work.

Finally, when Michelangelo was 13, his father reluctantly agreed to apprentice him to the Ghirlandajo brothers, well-known Florentine painters. Yet the boy remained unsatisfied because the brothers refused to teach him their art secrets. He played hooky and discovered the gardens of the Monastery of San Marco. Lorenzo the Magnificent, head of the house of Medici, had brought many ancient Greek and Roman statues to these gardens. As curator and teacher he installed a talented sculptor, Bertoldo di Giovanni.

Without his father's knowledge or permission, Michelangelo went to work under Bertoldo. One day Lorenzo himself saw the boy carving a marble faun's head. Lorenzo liked it so much that he took Michelangelo to live with him in his palace. He treated the boy like a son.

Lorenzo died in 1492, and Michelangelo grieved for him. Then Florence changed almost overnight. Fra Girolamo Savonarola, a Dominican monk, rose to power and held all the people under the spell of his sermons. Michelangelo feared Savonarola's influence and decided to leave Florence.

BRILLIANT SCULPTOR

In 1496 Michelangelo was in Rome for the first time. There he was commissioned to carve a Pietà. This was a marble group showing the Virgin Mary supporting the dead Christ on her knees. This superb sculpture, known as the *Madonna della Pietà*, won him wide fame. One of the few works signed by Michelangelo, it now stands in St. Peter's Basilica in Rome.

When he was 26 Michelangelo returned to Florence. He was given an 18-foot (5.5-meter) marble block that another sculptor had already started to carve. The block was nearly ruined. Michelangelo worked on it for more than two years. Out of its huge mass, and in spite of the difficulties caused by the first sculptor's work, he carved his youthful, courageous *David*, one of the world's greatest statues.

In 1505 Michelangelo was again in Rome. He was to work on a tomb for Pope Julius II. It was to be a giant structure, with some 40 statues arranged in three tiers. He spent months at Carrara selecting the marble. But shifting orders from the pope, political changes, jealousies, and new plans after the pope's death interfered with his work. Forty years later he had finished only a few figures. Among them were the majestic *Moses*, one of his most powerful works, which is now in the church of San Pietro in Vincoli, and the *Bound Slave*, now in the Louvre.

THE SISTINE CHAPEL FRESCOES

Between 1508 and 1512 Michelangelo painted the vaulted ceiling of the Sistine Chapel in Rome with hundreds of giant figures that made up his vision of the world's creation. He worked on a scaffold 60 feet (18 meters) above the floor and covered 10,000 square feet (930 square meters) of surface. Most times he painted lying on his back in a tight, cramped position. Each day fresh plaster was laid over a part of the ceiling. Michelangelo then had to complete that portion while the plaster was still wet. He could not repaint mistakes. Except for a man who laid the plaster and another who ground and mixed the paints, Michelangelo completed the whole fresco painting by himself.

The nine main scenes depict the story of Genesis from the Creation to the Flood. Other scenes show the ancestry of Christ, stirring moments in Bible history, and the Hebrew prophets and pagan gods dreaming of the good that was coming to the world. The painting is huge and majestic in every detail.

More than 20 years after he completed his ceiling frescoes for the Sistine Chapel, Michelangelo began his enormous fresco *The Last Judgment*. This is a vast painting that covers the entire wall of the chapel behind the altar. Its size, technical excellence, and the daring of its conception make it a worthy partner for the ceiling paintings.

WORK IN OTHER FIELDS

Painting and sculpture did not absorb all Michelangelo's genius. He had great talent in many fields. When his beloved Florence was in danger of attack, he superintended its fortification. He also wrote many sonnets that in their vigor and beauty recall his work in marble. Many were written in his old age to Vittoria Colonna, a lady of great beauty and intelligence.

In his last years he designed the dome of St. Peter's Basilica in Rome. This has been called the finest architectural achievement of the Italian Renaissance. He died on Feb. 18, 1564, at the age of 89 and was buried in the church of Santa Croce in Florence.

Michelangelo worked with many of the leaders of his time, the popes and the rulers of the Italian city-states. He knew and competed with Leonardo da Vinci and Raphael, two other creative geniuses who were his contemporaries. Except for Titian, Michelangelo was the last great man of Italy's golden age of art. He typified the vigor of mind and body, the energy, the spirit, and the combination of worldliness and religious zeal that marked that great period.

CLAUDE MONET

(b. 1840–d. 1926)

The leader of the 19th-century impressionist art movement, Claude Monet continued throughout his long career to pursue its goals. Monet preferred to paint outdoors, directly from nature. Almost all his work shows his desire to capture on canvas the changing effects of light.

Monet was born in Paris on Nov. 14, 1840, and spent his youth in Le Havre, where his father worked as a grocer. In 1859 Monet went to Paris to begin the serious study of art. In 1862, after an interval of military service, he returned to Paris and entered the studio of Charles Gleyre.

There he met Pierre Auguste Renoir, Alfred Sisley, and Jean-Frédéric Bazille. Soon, however, the four left Gleyre, and Monet led them on an expedition to the Fontainebleau Forest, where he introduced them to open-air painting.

After gaining acceptance into the Salons of 1865 and 1866, Monet suffered a series of reversals. He was deep in debt, and his huge painting *Women in the Garden* was rejected at the 1867 Salon. That same year his mistress, Camille Doncieux, gave birth to their first child, a son, Jean. Without a permanent home or an income, Monet lodged with friends and borrowed what money he could. At times he was even too poor to buy paint or canvas. In 1870 Claude and Camille were married. Their financial situation became worse during the next few years. Camille's health declined following the birth of their second son, Michel, and in 1879 she died.

In the spring of 1874 Monet and some of his friends decided to have a showing of their works. Among the exhibitors were Paul Cézanne, Edgar Degas, Renoir, Sisley, and Camille Pissarro. The group became known as "impressionists," a term applied derisively by a critic who said that Monet's sketchy landscape *Impression: Sunrise* (1872) reminded him of wallpaper. Although the exhibit attracted attention, none of the paintings was sold.

It was not until after 1886 that Monet began to enjoy his first financial success, a result of a growing market for his works in the United States. In the 1890s Monet painted several series of works— *Haystacks*, *Poplars*, and *Rouen Cathedral*—in which he rendered a single scene again and again, in all its variations of light, shadow, and season.

In 1892 Monet married Alice Hoschedé, the widow of a former friend and benefactor. They settled at Giverny, where Monet created the beautiful water garden that figures so prominently in his later paintings. Between 1899 and 1904 Monet traveled to London, where he painted his Thames series. In 1908 and 1909 he went to Venice, where he recorded the canals and palaces of that city in a series of paintings that he continued working on at Giverny until 1912. Aside from these trips, Monet remained at Giverny, where he continued painting until his death on Dec. 5, 1926, at the age of 86. His home and gardens at Giverny is now a national monument.

Impressionism, as developed by Monet, sought to capture the fleeting, momentary aspects of nature, especially to convey the atmospheric effects of light. As he pursued this goal, his technique became increasingly free, causing critics to remark that the paintings looked unfinished. Instead of mixing colors on his palette, Monet applied separate strokes of pure, unmixed color directly to the canvas. The method produced a shimmering, vibrating effect that simulated the effects of natural light. In his last paintings, the *Water Lilies* (1900–26), nature as a subject began to be less significant than color.

JUAN MARTÍNEZ MONTAÑÉS

(b. 1568–d. 1649)

Juan Martínez Montañés was a Spanish sculptor who was instrumental in the transition from Mannerism to the Baroque. His work influenced not only the sculptors and altar makers of Spain and Latin America but also the Spanish painters of his century.

Juan Martínez Montañés was born Juan de Martínez Montañés on March 16, 1568 in Alcalá la Real, Jaén, Spain. After studying in Granada under Pablo de Rojas (1579–82), Montañés went to Sevilla (Seville) in 1587 and established a studio that lasted until his death. He became known as the "Dios de la Madera" (God of Wood Carving) and had 50 years of enormous output and influence. He is remembered for his wood altars and altar figures covered with polished gold and paint in various colors. They are marked by an admirable aristocratic dignity, realistic yet idealized. He set the style throughout Spain and Latin America with such works as the statues of Christ on the cross, looking at the beholder; of the child Christ; and of the Immaculate Conception (all at the Sevilla Cathedral). The church in Santiponce, near Sevilla, contains his finest altar (1610–13); his largest work is at San Miguel in Jérez de la Frontera (1617–45). He died on June 18, 1649 in Sevilla.

BERTHE MORISOT

(b. 1841–d. 1895)

French impressionist artist Berthe Morisot was a painter and print-maker. A sister-in-law and protégée of Édouard Manet, she exhibited regularly with the impressionists and participated in their struggle for recognition.

The daughter of a wealthy government official—and a granddaughter of the Rococo painter Jean-Honoré Fragonard—Morisot was born on Jan. 14, 1841, in Bourges, France. Privately trained in art as a child, she showed unusual talent and determination. From 1862 to 1868 she worked under the guidance of the landscape painter Camille Corot. Starting in 1864 her paintings were regularly accepted at the government-sponsored annual art exhibit known as the Salon. In 1868 she met the innovative painter Édouard Manet, who was to exert a tremendous influence over her work. He did several portraits of her including *Repose* (in about 1870). Manet had a liberating effect on her work, and she in turn aroused his interest in outdoor painting. Morisot later married Manet's younger brother Eugène. An active participant in the first impressionist exhibition in 1874, she never

Painter and printmaker Berthe Morisot, a leading French impressionist whose life and works were influenced by Édouard Manet. The Bridgeman Art Library/Getty Images

again exhibited at the Salon. She had a reputation for culture and charm, counting many close friends among the artistic and literary elite of Paris. Morisot died there on March 2, 1895.

Morisot's paintings are delicate and subtle, exquisite in color, often with a subdued emerald glow. She frequently used her own family as subjects, particularly her sister Edma, who was portrayed in the works *The Artist's Sister, Mme Pontillon, Seated on the Grass* (1873) and *The Artist's Sister Edma and Their Mother* (1870). Her work was slow to find critical acceptance. However, she was at least as successful commercially during her lifetime as most of her peers in the impressionist movement.

EDVARD MUNCH

(b. 1863–d. 1944)

The Norwegian painter and printmaker Edvard Munch not only was his country's greatest artist, but he also greatly influenced the development of the artistic style known as German expressionism. In that style, the artist seeks to portray subjective emotions and responses to the world, rather than realistic depictions of its objects and events. His work often included the symbolic portrayal of such themes as misery, sickness, and death. *The Scream*, or *The Cry* (1893), probably his most familiar painting, is typical in its anguished expression of isolation and fear. (The two earliest versions of *The Scream* date to 1893; Munch created another version in 1895 and completed a fourth likely in 1910.)

Munch was born on Dec. 12, 1863, in Løten, Norway. He grew up in Christiania (now Oslo) and studied art under Christian Krohg, a Norwegian naturalistic painter. Munch's parents, a brother, and a sister died while he was still young, which probably contributed to the bleakness of much of his work. Paintings such as *The Sick Child* (1885–86), *Vampire* (1893–94), and *Ashes* (1894) show his preoccupation with the darker aspects of life.

Munch traveled to Paris in 1885, and his work began to show the influence of French painters—first, the impressionists, and then the postimpressionists—as well as art nouveau design. In 1892 he took part in an exhibit in Berlin; the violent emotion and unconventional imagery of the paintings he displayed in it stirred a great controversy. The scandal helped him to become more widely known.

Munch's circle of friends included several writers, one of whom was the Norwegian playwright Henrik Ibsen. Munch designed the sets for several of Ibsen's plays.

Between 1892 and 1908, Munch spent much of his time in Paris and Berlin, where he became known for his prints—etchings, lithographs, and woodcuts. After 1910 Munch returned to Norway, where he lived and painted until his death. In his later paintings Munch showed more interest in nature, and his work became more colorful and less grim. Munch died in Ekely, near Oslo, on January 23, 1944. He left many of his works to the city of Oslo, which built a museum in his honor.

NICCOLÒ DELL'ARCA

(b. 1435-1440?–d. 1494)

Niccolò dell'Arca was an early Renaissance sculptor famed for his intensely expressionistic use of realism combined with southern Classicism and a plastic naturalism typical of the Burgundian School and especially the work of Claus Sluter. The Ragusa, Bari, and Apulia variants of his name suggest that he might have come from southern Italy.

Niccolò, also called Niccolò d'Apulia, Niccolò da Ragusa, Nichollò de Bari, and Nicolaus de Apulia, was born probably some time between 1435 and 1440. He took his name from the monumental tomb (*arca* in Italian) of St. Dominic in the church of San Domenico, Bologna, where he made the canopy and most of the freestanding figures (1469–94). Three of the figures were later added by Michelangelo. His most famous work, the passionately dramatic *Lamentation over the Dead Christ* (seven freestanding polychrome terra-cotta figures, Santa Maria della Vita, Bologna, completed either 1462–63 or *c.* 1485) may have been inspired by similar groups by Guido Mazzoni.

Another terra-cotta sculpture group of the Virgin and Saints is the *Madonna di Piazza* (*c.* 1478) located above the main entrance of the Palazzo Comunale in Bologna. He died in 1494 in Bologna.

JOSEPH NOLLEKENS

(b. 1737–d. 1823)

Joseph Nollekens was a neoclassical sculptor whose busts made him the most fashionable English portrait sculptor of his day.

At 13 Nollekens entered the studio of the noted sculptor of tombs and busts Peter Scheemakers, from whom Nollekens learned to appreciate the sculpture of antiquity. In 1760 he went to Rome, where David Garrick and Laurence Sterne were among the English visitors who sat for him. After his return to England in 1770 he became a member of the Royal Academy (1772) and was patronized by George III. Among his famous likenesses are those of George III, William Pitt, Charles James Fox, and Benjamin West. Many of his works were influenced by ancient Roman busts of the late Republic style. He personally preferred sculpting mythological works based on ancient prototypes, especially genteel but erotic Venuses delicately modeled in an almost Rococo manner. Nollekens died on April 23, 1823, in London.

GEORGIA O'KEEFE

(b. 1887–d. 1986)

The career of painter Georgia O'Keeffe spanned the history of modern art. She is best known for semi-abstractions inspired by the bleak but colorful landscapes of New Mexico.

O'Keeffe was born near Sun Prairie, Wis., on Nov. 15, 1887. She grew up on her family's farm and left home to study at the Art Institute of Chicago in 1904. She subsequently studied at the Art Students League of New York, the University of Virginia, and Columbia University in New York City.

From 1913 to 1918 she supported herself by teaching art at the University of Virginia, Columbia College in South Carolina, and West Texas Normal College. She was also supervisor of art in the Amarillo, Tex., public schools. After 1918 she devoted herself entirely to painting.

Portrait of American abstract artist Georgia O'Keefe. Joe Munroe//Time & Life Pictures/ Getty Images

In 1916 a friend had shown some of O'Keeffe's work to photographer Alfred Stieglitz, who exhibited the drawings at his 291 Gallery in New York City. When she moved to New York in 1918 she was introduced to Stieglitz. They were married in 1924.

O'Keeffe's earliest paintings were abstract, but in the early 1920s she began painting large flowers and animal bones, subjects with which she became especially associated. She also did realistic scenes of New York and of the East River.

It was a trip to New Mexico in 1929 that led her to the semiabstract style for which she became famous. She usually spent the summers there and the winters in New York City or at Lake George, N.Y. Stieglitz died in 1946, and after that O'Keeffe began to travel more widely. She went around the world in 1959, and from the trip came a series of paintings based on her views of earth, sky, and clouds. Her autobiography, *Georgia O'Keeffe*, was published in 1976. She died in Santa Fe, N.M., on March 6, 1986.

PHIDIAS

(b. 490?–d. 430? BCE)

The Athenian sculptor Phidias, who directed the building of the Parthenon and the statues of the gods, initiated the Greek classical

style of art. He alone, it was said, had seen the gods and made them visible to others.

Phidias was born in Athens in about 490 BCE. His earliest works include a bronze statue of Athena to celebrate the victory of the Greeks over the Persians at the battle of Marathon. In about 456 BCE the statue was placed on the Acropolis in Athens. About 30 feet (9 meters) high, it was the largest statue yet erected in Athens.

The Persians had twice invaded Athens and sacked the city, forcing the Athenians to flee. On their return the Athenians had found their homes and temples destroyed. Everything on the Acropolis was smashed and all its defenders killed. The statesman Pericles persuaded the Athenian assembly to undertake a great building program, and in 447 BCE Pericles appointed Phidias artistic director to superintend the rebuilding. Phidias designed and supervised the building of the Parthenon, the magnificent temple of Athena on the Acropolis. He himself made the gold and ivory statue of Athena that stood inside the Parthenon and that was dedicated to the goddess in 438 BCE. He also designed the 92 relief carvings along the outside as well as the frieze that extended around the top of the walls.

Phidias's last years remain a mystery. In 432 BCE Pericles's enemies accused Phidias of stealing gold from the statue of Athena, but Phidias had applied the gold in such a way that he was able to peel it off and prove that none was missing. They then accused him of impiety for including portraits of himself and Pericles on the shield of Athena. It was thought that he might have died shortly thereafter in prison, but now it is believed that he was exiled to Elis, where he created the statue of the Olympian Zeus. This masterpiece, a huge statue of Zeus for the Olympian temple in Elis, was one of the seven wonders of the ancient world.

PABLO PICASSO

(b. 1881–d. 1973)

The reaction in the late 19th century against naturalism in art led to a sequence of different movements in the 20th century. In each of

Spanish artist Pablo Picasso, relaxing at home in the 1960s. Paul Popper/
Popperfoto/Getty Images

these periods of innovation Pablo Picasso played an important part. Primarily a painter, he also became a fine sculptor, engraver, and ceramist.

Pablo Ruiz y Picasso was born on Oct. 25, 1881, in Málaga, on
the Mediterranean coast of Spain. His father, an art teacher, early
recognized his son's genius. Picasso studied at the Academy of Fine Arts
in Barcelona, where his father was appointed professor in 1896. Pablo
had already mastered realistic technique, however, and had little use for
school. At 16 he had his own studio in Barcelona. In 1900 he first visited
Paris, and in 1904 he settled there.

Picasso's personal style began to form in the years from 1901 to 1904,
a period often referred to as his blue period because of the pervasive
blue tones he used in his paintings at that time. In 1905, as he became

more successful, Picasso altered his palette, and the blue tones gave way to a terra-cotta color, a shade of deep pinkish red. At the same time his subject matter grew less melancholy and included dancers, acrobats, and harlequins. The paintings he did during the years between 1905 and 1907 are said to belong to his rose period.

In 1907 Picasso struck off in an entirely different direction with *Les Demoiselles d'Avignon*. This painting shows the influence of his new fascination with primitive art and carvings, especially those of African origin. The picture represents a major turning point in art because it opened the door to cubism and the later abstract movement. Working with his friend and fellow painter Georges Braque, Picasso began experimenting with increasingly analytical and geometric forms. His painting *The Three Musicians*, which dates from 1921, is one of his major achievements using this technique.

In 1917 Picasso had gone to Rome to design costumes and scenery for Sergey Diaghilev's Ballets Russes. This work stimulated another departure in Picasso's work, and he began to paint the works now referred to as belonging to his classic period, which lasted from about 1918 until 1925.

At the same time he was working on designs for the ballet, Picasso also continued to develop the cubist technique, making it less rigorous and austere. By the time he painted *Guernica*, his moving vision of the Spanish Civil War, the straight lines of early cubism had given way to curved forms. This huge painting, considered by many to be his masterpiece, was Picasso's response to the 1937 bombing by the Fascist forces of the small Basque town of Guernica. He completed this emotional political statement in the same year. In it, as in many of his later pictures, distortions of form approach surrealism, but Picasso never called himself a surrealist.

From about 1904, shortly after he settled in Paris, until 1911, Picasso had lived with Fernande Olivier, who may have inspired the sunnier outlook reflected in his rose period. From about 1911 until her death in 1917, he lived with Marcelle Humbert. In 1918 Picasso married a young Russian ballerina, Olga Koklova. The couple, who later separated and were divorced in 1935, had one son, Paulo. Olga died in 1955. In 1961, at the age of 80, the artist married his model, Jacqueline Roque.

Picasso remained in France throughout World War II, but he was forbidden to exhibit his work after the German occupation. He joined the French Communist party in 1944. In 1955 he moved to the French Riviera.

Picasso continued to work with incredible speed and versatility—as painter, ceramist, sculptor, designer, and graphic artist—into his 90s. The value of his estate was estimated at more than 500 million dollars when he died on April 8, 1973, in Mougins, France.

GERMAIN PILON

(b. 1535–d. 1590)

Germain Pilon was French sculptor whose work, principally monumental tombs, is a transitional link between the Gothic tradition and the sculpture of the Baroque period.

Pilon was born in 1535 in Paris. A sculptor's son, he was employed at age 20 on the decoration of the tomb of King Francis I at Saint-Denis. His earlier work clearly shows an Italian influence, but eventually he developed a more distinctively French expression by fusing elements from classical art, Gothic sculpture, and Michelangelo with the Fontainebleau adaptation of Mannerism, a style characterized by subjective conceptions, studied elegance, and virtuoso artifice.

Pilon's best-known works are funerary sculptures for Henry II. It was a custom of the period for men of high estate to assign their remains to more than one burial site—often one for the body, one for the heart, and one for the entrails. Pilon's monument for the heart of Henry II (c. 1561) consists of three marble Graces of great elegance supporting an urn. It was perhaps based on a design by Primaticcio. For the principal tomb of Henry II and Catherine de Médicis at Saint-Denis (1563–70), also designed by Primaticcio, Pilon created four bronze corner figures and kneeling figures of the king and queen in bronze. Most important, however, are the seminude, marble gisants, or figures of the royal pair reclining in death. Considered by some to be his most sublime achievement, the gisants are a Renaissance idealization of a Gothic convention and possess a depth of emotion that Pilon perhaps never again reached.

Sculptor royal from 1568, Pilon had a successful career as a portraitist, his finest work in the genre being the kneeling figure of René de Birague (1583–85). Pilon also created an effigy, *Valentine Balbiani*, of Birague's wife. It is also believed that his bronze relief *Deposition* was created for Birague's private chapel. Appointed controller of the mint in 1572, he contributed to French medal casting a distinguished series of bronze medallions in 1575. Pilon was commissioned to decorate the Valois Chapel (1559, destroyed 1719) in Saint-Denis Abbey, and he worked on several marble statues, among them *Risen Christ* (begun 1572), that were probably intended for the chapel but were unfinished at the time of his death in 1590.

HORACE PIPPIN

(b. 1888–d. 1946)

Horace Pippin was an American folk painter known for his depictions of African American life and the horrors of war.

Pippin was born Feb. 22, 1888, in West Chester, Pa. His childhood was spent in Goshen, N.Y., a town that sometimes appears in his paintings. There he drew horses at the local racetrack and, according to his own account, painted biblical scenes on frayed pieces of muslin. He was variously employed as an ironworker, junk dealer, and porter, until World War I, when he served in the infantry. He was wounded in 1918 and discharged with a partially paralyzed right arm. He settled in West Chester, and eventually began to paint by burning designs into wood panels with a red-hot poker and then painting in the outlined areas.

His first large canvas was an eloquent protest against war, *End of the War: Starting Home* (1931–34), which was followed by other antiwar pictures, such as *Shell Holes and Observation Balloon* (1931) and many versions of *Holy Mountain* (all from *c.* 1944–45). His most frequently used theme centered on the African American experience, as seen in his series entitled *Cabin in the Cotton* (mid-1930s) and his paintings of episodes in the lives of the antislavery leader John Brown and Abraham Lincoln.

After the art world discovered Pippin in 1937, these pictures in particular brought him wide acclaim as the greatest black painter of his time. He enjoyed the enthusiastic support of art collectors Christian Brinton, Albert C. Barnes, and Edith Halpert, owner of the New York Gallery in New York City. His work was featured in the landmark exhibition "Masters of Popular Painting," held at the Museum of Modern Art in New York in 1938. Pippin also executed portraits and biblical subjects. His early works are characterized by their heavy and thick use of paint (a style known as impasto) and restricted use of color. His later works are more precisely painted in a bolder palette. Pippin died on July 6, 1946, in West Chester.

JACKSON POLLOCK

(b. 1912–d. 1956)

Nicknamed Jack the Dripper for his unique style of painting, the American artist Jackson Pollock created his trademark murals by tacking a large canvas to the floor and using a stick to drip or splash paint from all four sides of the canvas. His style caused a critical controversy, and his use of painting for total personal expression—known as abstract expressionism—was widely imitated by later generations of artists.

Paul Jackson Pollock was born on Jan. 28, 1912, in Cody, Wyo., and grew up in California and Arizona. In 1930 Pollock moved to New York City and enrolled in the Art Students League. He studied under Thomas Hart Benton, whose realistic style of painting he later rejected. During the 1930s Pollock rode freight trains cross-country and sketched the landscapes he observed. In 1935 he was employed by the Federal Art Project.

Pollock's early paintings rely on powerful imagery and reflect the influence of Pablo Picasso and the Mexican muralist José Clemente Orozco. After his first one-man show in 1943, Pollock held shows of new works nearly every year, including exhibitions in Venice, Milan, and Paris. By the late 1940s he abandoned his easel and brush. Instead he dripped enamel or aluminum paint in a manner that earned the label

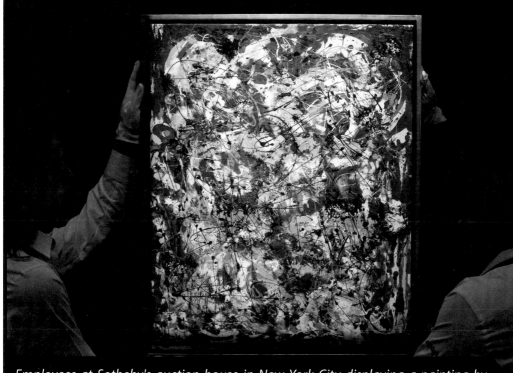

Employees at Sotheby's auction house in New York City displaying a painting by Jackson Pollock during a 2012 sale. Peter Macdiarmid/Getty Images

action painting. Pollock's technique resulted in canvases covered with complex linear patterns woven together in multiple layers. In his later works faces and familiar shapes are recognizable behind the mass of lines. In the early 1950s Pollock painted almost exclusively in black, brown, and white. Among his best-known works are *Full Fathom Five*, *Autumn Rhythm*, *Easter and the Totem*, and *Blue Poles*.

Pollock died in an automobile accident in East Hampton, N.Y., on Aug. 11, 1956. Pollock's fame did not bring him wealth during his lifetime, but his paintings have sold for some of the highest prices paid for works by an American artist. *Lavender Mist*, which the artist sold for 1,500 dollars when he painted it in 1950, was purchased by the National Gallery of Art for more than 2 million dollars in 1976.

PIERRE PUGET

(b. 1620–d. 1694)

French painter and architect Pierre Puget was one of the most original of the French Baroque sculptors. He was able to evoke drama and emotion, such as pain and anguish, in his sculptures.

Born on Oct. 16, 1620, in or near Marseille, France, Puget traveled to Italy in 1640–43, where he was employed by a muralist, Pietro da Cortona, to work on the ceiling decorations of the Barberini Palace in Rome and the Pitti Palace in Florence. Between 1643 and 1656 he was active in Marseille and Toulon chiefly as a painter, but he also carved colossal figureheads for men-of-war. He received an important sculpture commission in 1656 for the doorway of the Hôtel de Ville, Toulon; his caryatid figures there, although in the tradition of Roman Baroque, show a strain and an anguish that are similar to the Mannerist works of Michelangelo. Such feelings are passionately expressed in works such as *Milo of Croton* (c. 1671–84), in which the athlete Milo, whose hand is caught in a tree stump, is portrayed under attack by a lion.

In 1659 Puget went to Paris, where he attracted the attention of Louis XIV's minister Nicolas Fouquet. The latter fell from power in 1661 while Puget was in Italy selecting marble for the Hercules statue commissioned by him (now the *Hercule gaulois* in the Louvre). Puget remained in Italy for several years, establishing a considerable reputation as a sculptor in Genoa. *St. Sebastian* in Sta. Maria di Carignano is among his best works there.

After 1669 Puget's life was spent mainly in Toulon and Marseille, where he was engaged in architectural work and the decoration of ships as well as sculpture. His *Milo of Croton* was taken to Versailles in 1683, and *Perseus and Andromeda* was well received there the next year. Puget, however, was soon the victim of intrigues by his rivals, and his success at court was short-lived. Other works planned for Versailles were either refused or frustrated, and Puget became embittered by these failures. He died on December 2, 1694, in Marseille.

RAPHAEL

(b. 1483–d. 1520)

As a master painter and architect of the Italian High Renaissance, Raphael produced works that rivaled the well-known masterpieces of Leonardo da Vinci and Michelangelo. His later works used a new style that tended toward the baroque. His architecture displayed the exaggerated scale and abnormal forms of Mannerism.

Rafaello Sanzio was born on April 6, 1483, in Urbino, Italy. His father, Giovanni Santi, was a minor painter and poet who died when Raphael was 11. Later the boy went to Perugia as an apprentice to his father's friend, the painter Perugino. Gradually he became a greater artist than his teacher. From 1504 to 1508 Raphael spent most of his time in Florence. In this great cultural center he met Michelangelo, Leonardo da Vinci, and Fra Bartolommeo. He studied and copied the works of these and other artists and quickly absorbed the new Florentine style. His works from this period were chiefly Madonnas—gentle, graceful, and beautiful creations, more idealized than realistic. Among the most famous are *Madonna of the Goldfinch*, *Madonna and Child Enthroned with Saints*, *Esterházy Madonna*, *Ansidei Madonna*, and *La Belle Jardinière*. In his lifetime Raphael painted more than 300 pictures on the Madonna theme.

Raphael spent the last 12 years of his life in Rome. He was called to the city in 1508, when Pope Julius II decided to have certain rooms in the Vatican redecorated. When he saw Raphael's sketches, he commissioned the young artist to redecorate with frescoes the walls of four rooms in the pope's private apartments, the Stanza della Segnatura. In these murals Raphael showed his genius for grouping crowds of magnificent figures. He is at his best in the *School of Athens* and the *Disputa*. The *School of Athens* shows Plato and Aristotle surrounded by philosophers, past and present. It illustrates the continuity of Platonic thought. The *Disputa* shows a vision of God and the prophets and apostles above a group of representatives of the Roman Catholic Church.

Julius II died in 1513. His successor, Leo X, appointed Raphael to work alongside Donato Bramante in the rebuilding of St. Peter's Basilica. Following the death of Bramante, Leo made Raphael chief architect on the project. Leo commissioned Raphael to make full-scale cartoons for ten tapestries that were woven in Brussels for the Sistine Chapel. He was appointed commissioner of antiquities for the city, and he drew an archaeological map of Rome. In his later years Raphael painted portraits. The best known are *Pope Julius II* and *Baldassare Castiglione*. With Michelangelo and Leonardo, Raphael is regarded as one of the three great painters in whom the Italian Renaissance flowered. He died in Rome on his 37th birthday, April 6, 1520.

ROBERT RAUSCHENBERG

(b. 1925–d. 2008)

U.S. painter and sculptor Robert Rauschenberg is considered one of the major artists of the latter half of the 20th century. During his early career he devised new techniques of three-dimensional collage and assemblage. Within his artwork Rauschenberg used subject matter drawn from the popular culture, history, and mass media of the United States. His use of images and commonplace objects from the popular culture made him one of the forerunners of the pop art movement.

He was born Milton Rauschenberg on Oct. 22, 1925, in Port Arthur, Tex. Drafted into the U.S. Navy, he trained to be a neuropsychiatric technician. While in the service during World War II, Rauschenberg visited the Huntington Art Gallery in San Marino, Calif. The artworks in the collection made a strong impression on him and stimulated his interest in making art. Once discharged from the navy, he studied painting at the Kansas City Art Institute in 1946–47. During this period he changed his name from Milton to Robert. Rauschenberg traveled to Paris in 1948 to study at the Académie Julien but returned home within the year. From 1948 to 1950 he studied at Black Mountain College in North Carolina, under Josef Albers, and at the Art Students League in New York City.

Some of Rauschenberg's first artworks in the early 1950s were a series of all-white paintings and a series of all-black paintings. In subsequent works he began to make art with such objects as Coca-Cola bottles, traffic barricades, and stuffed birds, calling them "combine" paintings— a combination of sculpture and painting. His combines were inspired by the work of the Dada artists, especially Marcel Duchamp. One of Rauschenberg's most famous combines, *Monogram* (1959), consists of a stuffed Angora goat with an automobile tire around its midsection.

In 1954 Rauschenberg met a young painter named Jasper Johns. During their friendship, they discussed art, critiqued each other's work, and eventually had their art represented by the same gallery in New York City. Their early artwork incorporated some of the ideas that would later become central to pop art, primarily the use of imagery from U.S. popular culture. Interested in collaborating with other artists, Rauschenberg began to work with modern dancer and choreographer Merce Cunningham, an associate from Black Mountain College. He started as a designer of costumes and sets and later worked as a technical director for the Merce Cunningham Dance Company. He also produced theatrical pieces with composer John Cage, another close friend from Black Mountain College.

From the late 1950s Rauschenberg experimented with the use of newspaper and magazine photographs in his paintings. He devised a process using solvent to transfer images directly onto the canvas. In the early 1960s he used Andy Warhol's silk-screen stencil technique for applying photographic images to large expanses of canvas. After transferring the images to the canvas, Rauschenberg visually reinforced the images and unified their composition with broad strokes of paint reminiscent of abstract expressionist brushwork. These works draw on themes from modern U.S. history and popular culture and are notable for their sophisticated compositions and the spatial relations of the objects depicted in them. Two of his silk-screen paintings from 1964, *Axle* and *Retroactive*, use the image of U.S. President John F. Kennedy. In the same year, Rauschenberg became the first U.S. artist to win the grand prize at the prestigious Venice Biennale.

From the 1970s some of Rauschenberg's works were influenced by visits with artists in such countries as China, Japan, and Mexico.

Rauschenberg continued to explore the possibilities of lithography and other printmaking techniques, making prints on silk, cotton, and cheesecloth. He created three-dimensional constructions of cloth, paper, and bamboo in an Asian style. In addition to using imagery from the commercial print media, he also began to rely more heavily on his own photography.

Among Rauschenberg's other interests were artists' rights and the promotion of art across cultural and political borders. In 1966 Rauschenberg and scientist Billy Klüver established Experiments in Art and Technology (EAT), a foundation that cultivated the collaboration of artists and scientists. In the early 1970s he established Change, Inc., in order to provide funds for artists in need.

Inspired by his earlier travels, Rauschenberg announced the formation of the Rauschenberg Overseas Culture Interchange (ROCI) in 1984. During the six years of ROCI's existence, Rauschenberg exhibited artwork in North and South America, Asia, the Caribbean, the Soviet Union (now Russia), and Europe. The subject matter of the artworks he created during his travels with ROCI incorporated the cultural images of the countries he had visited. These works were displayed in 1991 at the National Gallery of Art in Washington, D.C. A major retrospective of Rauschenberg's art career was exhibited in New York City's Solomon R. Guggenheim Museum in 1997. He died in Captiva Island, Fla., on May 12, 2008.

MAN RAY

(b. 1890–d. 1976)

A U.S. painter and photographer, Man Ray was a tireless experimenter who participated in the cubist, dadaist, and surrealist art movements. Ray was born on Aug. 27, 1890, in Philadelphia, Pa. He worked most of his life in Paris, France, creating camera-less pictures, or photograms, which he called rayographs, and he was the first to use the technique of solarization for aesthetic purposes. His work was known for its odd juxtapositions. Ray became internationally famous as a fashion and portrait photographer. In 1961 he was awarded the Gold

Medal at the Photography Biennale, Venice, and he received the German Photographic Society Cultural award in 1966. He died on Nov. 18, 1976.

REMBRANDT

(b. 1606–d. 1669)

The greatest artist of the Dutch school was Rembrandt. He was a master of light and shadow whose paintings, drawings, and etchings made him a giant in the history of art.

Rembrandt Harmenszoon van Rijn was born on July 15, 1606, in Leiden, the Netherlands. His father was a miller who wanted the boy to follow a learned profession, but Rembrandt left the University of Leiden to study painting. His early work was devoted to showing the lines, light and shade, and color of the people he saw about him. He was influenced by the work of Caravaggio and was fascinated by the work of many other Italian artists. When Rembrandt became established as a painter, he began to teach and continued teaching art throughout his life.

In 1631, when Rembrandt's work had become well known and his studio in Leiden was flourishing, he moved to Amsterdam. He became the leading portrait painter in Holland and received many commissions for portraits as well as for paintings of religious subjects. He lived the life of a wealthy, respected citizen and met the beautiful Saskia van Uylenburgh, whom he married in 1634. She was the model for many of his paintings and drawings. Rembrandt's works from this period are characterized by strong lighting effects. In addition to portraits, Rembrandt attained fame for his landscapes, while as an etcher he ranks among the foremost of all time. When he had no other model, he painted or sketched his own image. It is estimated that he painted between 50 and 60 self-portraits.

In 1636 Rembrandt began to depict quieter, more contemplative scenes with new warmth in color. During the next few years three of his four children died in infancy, and in 1642 his wife died. In the 1630s and 1640s he made many landscape drawings and etchings. His landscape paintings are imaginative, rich portrayals of the land around him. Rembrandt was at his most inventive in the work popularly known

Dutch master Rembrandt, rendered in a self-portrait of the artist as an older man.
Imagno/Hulton Fine Art Collection/Getty Images

as *The Night Watch*, painted in 1642. It depicts a group of city guards-men awaiting the command to fall in line. Each man is painted with the care that Rembrandt gave to single portraits, yet the composition is such that the separate figures are second in interest to the effect of the whole. The canvas is brilliant with color, movement, and light. In the foreground are two men, one in bright yellow, and the other in black. The shadow of one color tones down the lightness of the other. In the center of the painting is a little girl dressed in yellow.

Rembrandt had become accustomed to living comfortably. From the time he could afford to, he bought many paintings by other artists. By the mid-1650s he was living so far beyond his means that his house and his goods had to be auctioned to pay some of his debts. He had fewer commissions in the 1640s and 1650s, but his financial circumstances were not unbearable. For today's student of art, Rembrandt remains, as the Dutch painter Jozef Israels said, "the true type of artist, free, untrammeled by traditions."

The number of works attributed to Rembrandt varies. He produced approximately 600 paintings, 300 etchings, and 1,400 drawings. Some of his works are: *St. Paul in Prison* (1627); *Supper at Emmaus* (1630); *The Anatomy Lesson of Dr. Nicolaes Tulp* (1632); *Young Girl at an Open Half-Door* (1645); *The Mill* (1650); *Aristotle Contemplating the Bust of Homer* (1653); *The Return of the Prodigal Son* (after 1660); *The Syndics of the Drapers' Guild* (1662); and many portraits.

PIERRE-AUGUSTE RENOIR

(b. 1841–d. 1919)

The brilliant colors and beautiful, rounded figures of Renoir's paint-ings have never been equaled. He was one of the leaders of France's impressionist movement but later opted for a more formal style. His portraits, landscapes, and still lifes have a unique texture and light that places Renoir's work among that of the world's finest artists.

Pierre-Auguste Renoir was born on Feb. 25, 1841, in Limoges, France. His family moved to Paris when he was young. He showed artistic tal-ent early and became an apprentice in a porcelain factory when he was 13.

Portrait of Pierre-Auguste Renoir, who was a leader of France's 19th-century impressionist movement. Hulton Archive/Getty Images

There he learned to paint floral patterns on the porcelain. In 1862 he began studying with Swiss painter Charles Gleyre, whose other students included Claude Monet, Alfred Sisley, and Jean-Frédéric Bazille. They became friends and later joined Paul Cézanne and Camille Pissarro in an attempt to change the rigid formula that artists in their day were required to follow. These young artists wanted to reflect contemporary society in their works, and they did not want the state-operated salon to decide which paintings deserved to be exhibited and sold.

In 1874 Renoir was chosen by his friends to lead the first exhibition of their work. There Monet's painting *Impression: Sunrise* led cynical critics to label the group impressionists. In the next 12 years the impressionists had seven more exhibitions. Meanwhile, Renoir had become acquainted with the wealthy publisher Georges Charpentier, who commissioned portraits of his family. Charpentier also organized a personal exhibition for Renoir in 1879. In 1881 Renoir traveled to Algeria, Italy, and southeastern France. He abandoned the style that he had developed and began to paint in a more disciplined, classical way. He was influenced by the things he saw, including the frescoes in Pompeii and the Raphael paintings in Rome.

In 1890 (some sources say 1881) Renoir married Aline Charigot. They had three sons who appear often in Renoir's paintings. In 1894 Renoir suffered his first bout of rheumatoid arthritis. The disease was to plague him until the end of his life, but he painted until the very end. When he became ill he took his family to the milder climate of southern France.

In 1907 they settled permanently in Cagnes, and by 1910 Renoir could no longer walk. In 1915 Renoir's wife went to visit their son, who had been injured in World War I. She died soon after her return, and Renoir died four years later, on Dec. 3, 1919, in Cagnes.

His works include *The Theater Box* (1874), *Portrait of Monet* (1875), *Madame Charpentier and Her Children* (1878), *Two Little Circus Girls* (1879), *The Luncheon of the Boating Party* (1881), *Bathers* (1884–87), *Young Girl Reading* (1892), and *After the Bath* (about 1895).

FAITH RINGGOLD

(b. 1930–)

Faith Ringgold is American artist and author who became famous for innovative, quilted narrations that communicate her political beliefs.

Ringgold was born on Oct. 8, 1930, in New York, N.Y. She grew up in New York City's Harlem, and while still in high school she decided to be an artist. She attended City College of New York, where she received B.S. (1955) and M.A. (1959) degrees. In the mid-1950s she began teaching art in New York public schools. By the 1960s her work had matured, reflecting her burgeoning political consciousness, study of African arts and history, and appreciation for the freedom of form used by her young students.

In 1963 Ringgold began a body of paintings called the *American People* series, which portrays the civil rights movement from a female perspective. In the 1970s she created African-style masks, painted political posters, lectured frequently at feminist art conferences, and actively sought the racial integration of the New York art world. She originated a demonstration against the Whitney Museum of American Art and helped win admission for black artists to the exhibit schedule at the Museum of Modern Art. In 1970 she cofounded, with one of her daughters, the advocacy group Women Students and Artists for Black Art Liberation.

Among Ringgold's most renowned works, her "story quilts" were inspired by the Tibetan tankas (paintings framed in cloth) that she viewed on a visit to museums in Amsterdam. She painted these quilts with narrative images and original stories set in the context of African American history. Her mother frequently collaborated with her on these. Examples of this work includes *Who's Afraid of Aunt Jemima?* (1984), *Sonny's Quilt* (1986), and *Tar Beach* (1988), which Ringgold adapted into a children's book in 1991. The latter book, which was named Caldecott Honor Book in 1992, tells of a young black girl in New York City who dreams about flying. Ringgold's later books for children include *Aunt Harriet's Underground Railroad in the Sky* (1992) and *My Dream of Martin Luther King* (1995). Her memoirs, *We Flew over the Bridge*, were published in 1995.

DIEGO RIVERA

(b. 1886–d. 1957)

Mexican painter Diego Rivera, petting his dog, in the 1940s. Archive Photos/ Getty Images

Of the many controversies that embroiled the Mexican painter Diego Rivera because of the didactic character of his work, the removal in 1933 of his fresco *Man at the Crossroads* from Rockefeller Center in New York City is probably the best known. A Communist, the artist had included in his fresco a figure that resembled the Soviet leader Lenin. Although the public clamor that arose forced its removal, Rivera reproduced the fresco for the Palace of Fine Arts in Mexico City, Mexico.

Diego María Concepción Juan Nepomuceno Estanislao de la Rivera y Barrientos Acosta y Rodríguez was born on Dec. 8, 1886, in Guanajuato, Mexico.

Having received a government scholarship, Rivera studied for a time at the San Carlos Academy of Fine Arts, but he was expelled for his participation in student riots. He settled in Paris, France, in 1909 and became friends with Pablo Picasso and other leading modern painters. After exhibiting his work in Mexico in 1910, he returned to Paris and then toured Italy to study frescoes there.

Rivera returned to Mexico in 1921 and executed frescoes in Mexico City and Chapingo. His hope was to create a new national art based on revolutionary themes in the wake of the Mexican Revolution. After nine years working in Mexico, he spent 1930–34 painting murals in the United States. One done for the Detroit Institute of Arts in 1932 was criticized as irreligious, and, after the Rockefeller Center controversy the following year, Rivera was deemed too radical for further commissions in the United States.

Rivera's work remained popular in Mexico. He was working on his most ambitious project—a mural based on the history of Mexico for the National Palace in Mexico City—at the time of his death. He died in Mexico City on Nov. 25, 1957. Rivera was twice married to the Mexican painter Frida Kahlo.

NORMAN ROCKWELL

(b. 1894–d. 1978)

For more than 50 years no artist's works were better known to the American public than the paintings of Norman Rockwell. In 1916 he sold his first cover illustration to *The Saturday Evening Post*, and—by the time the magazine suspended publication in 1969—his paintings had decorated 317 of its covers. From 1926 until 1976 he illustrated the Boy Scout calendar. During World War II his posters depicting the Four Freedoms were printed and distributed by the Office of War Information. In 1977 Rockwell was awarded the Presidential Medal of Freedom by President Gerald Ford.

Rockwell was born in New York City on Feb. 3, 1894. At age 16 he left high school to study painting on a scholarship at the Art Students League in New York City. A teacher got him his first commissions, and

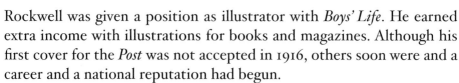

Rockwell was given a position as illustrator with *Boys' Life*. He earned extra income with illustrations for books and magazines. Although his first cover for the *Post* was not accepted in 1916, others soon were and a career and a national reputation had begun.

During the next several decades Rockwell also did covers and illustrations for *Ladies' Home Journal*, *McCall's*, and other magazines. He illustrated editions of Mark Twain's *Huckleberry Finn* and *Tom Sawyer*. Art critics did not appreciate his work for many years, and they regarded him merely as an illustrator—all he ever claimed to be. But the public loved his vignettes of small-town America, done with humor and warmth. His books of paintings all sold well. Among them were *Norman Rockwell, Illustrator*, published in 1946, *My Adventures as an Illustrator* (1960), *The Norman Rockwell Album* (1961), and *Norman Rockwell, Artist and Illustrator* (1970). His posters of the Four Seasons, like those of the Four Freedoms, were widely distributed. Rockwell died in Stockbridge, Mass., on Nov. 8, 1978.

AUGUSTE RODIN

(b. 1840–d. 1917)

The French artist Auguste Rodin had a profound influence on 20th-century sculpture. His works are distinguished by their stunning strength and realism. Rodin refused to ignore the negative aspects of humanity, and his works confront distress and moral weakness as well as passion and beauty.

François-Auguste-René Rodin was born on Nov. 12, 1840, in Paris. At the age of 14 he entered the Petite École, a school of decorative arts in Paris. He applied three times to study at the renowned École des Beaux-Arts but was rejected each time. In 1858 he began to do decorative stonework in order to make his living. Four years later the death of his sister Marie so traumatized Rodin that he entered a sacred order.

The father superior of the order recognized Rodin's talents and encouraged him to pursue his art. In 1864 Rodin met a seamstress named Rose Beuret. She became his life companion and was the model for many of his works. That year Rodin submitted his *Man with a Broken*

Nose to the Paris Salon. It was rejected but later accepted under the title *Portrait of a Roman*. Rodin traveled in 1875 to Italy, where the works of Michelangelo made a strong impression on him. The trip inspired his sculpture *The Age of Bronze*, which was exhibited at the Paris Salon in 1877. It caused a scandal because the critics could not believe that Rodin had not used a casting of a live model in creating so realistic a work.

The controversy brought Rodin more fame than praise might have. In 1880 he was commissioned to create a bronze door for the future Museum of Decorative Arts. Although the work was unfinished at the time of his death, it provided the basis for some of Rodin's most influential and powerful work. In 1884 he was commissioned to create a monument that became *The Burghers of Calais*. His statues *St. John the Baptist Preaching*, *Eve*, *The Age of Bronze*, and *The Thinker* are world famous. Rodin died on Nov. 17, 1917, and was buried at Meudon.

When Rodin was 76 years old he gave the French government the entire collection of his own works and other art objects he had acquired. They occupy the Hôtel Biron in Paris as the Musée Rodin and are still placed as Rodin set them.

MARK ROTHKO

(b. 1903–d. 1970)

The American painter Mark Rothko pioneered abstract expressionism, the most distinctive art movement in the United States in the mid-20th century. He began his career as a realist and moved gradually to increasingly abstract works. Eventually his works became monochromes, statements of what he called minimal art. His bold use of color led to the development of color field painting.

Marcus Rothkovitch was born in Dvinsk, Russia, on Sept. 25, 1903. His family moved to the United States in 1913 and settled in Portland, Ore. Rothko attended Yale University from 1921 to 1923 and spent a few months at the Art Students League in New York City in 1925. Apart from this he had no formal art training. The chief work of his realistic period, in the 1930s, was the Subway series showing the loneliness of city life. At this time he was working for the Federal Art Project run by

the federal government. By the early 1940s he was doing semiabstract paintings, but by 1948 he had arrived at purely abstract forms. His simple rectangles of glowing color were internationally acclaimed by the 1950s.

In 1961 there was a retrospective exhibit of his work at the Museum of Modern Art, an honor accorded very few artists. From 1958 until 1966 he worked on a series of 14 large canvases that were eventually placed in a chapel in Houston, Tex. Plagued by ill health and convinced he was being ignored by other artists, Rothko committed suicide on Feb. 25, 1970.

After his death the disposition of his paintings led to one of the most spectacular court cases in the history of art. He had hoarded 798 paintings. The executors of his estate and an art dealer were accused of profiting at the expense of his two children. The works were divided in 1979 between the children and the Mark Rothko Foundation. The foundation's paintings were later distributed among 19 museums.

HENRI ROUSSEAU

(b. 1844–d. 1910)

The French painter Henri Rousseau is usually described as a primitive, a term used to describe a self-taught painter whose technique lacks the polish of a trained artist. Proportions of figures may be in error, for example, as in a child's drawing. In Rousseau's work these qualities are far outweighed by his complex designs and color harmonies and by the strong influence of his imagination.

Henri Rousseau was born on May 21, 1844, in Laval, France, the son of a tinsmith. He left school at an early age and entered military service, where he stayed for four years. After his marriage in 1869, he became an inspector with the Paris toll office.

Rousseau began to paint seriously in about 1880, and in 1886 he exhibited his work for the first time. In 1893 he retired on a tiny pension and devoted himself to painting. He gave lessons in drawing and music to eke out a meager income. Meanwhile, he regularly exhibited paintings at the art shows organized by experimental painters. Critics and the public ridiculed his work. A number of young poets and painters who later became famous saw merit in his paintings, however, and encouraged him.

Rousseau was an innocent and unworldly man and these qualities enabled him to paint in a delightfully fresh way. His most famous pictures depict scenes of exotic jungles of outsize plants. In the lush, light-filtered foliage, mysterious eyes glitter and lions attack their prey. *The Sleeping Gypsy*, painted in 1897, shows a moonlit desert scene of a Roma (Gypsy) woman and a lion. *The Dream* (1910), in which a woman reclines on a red velvet sofa in the jungle while a snake charmer plays a horn, has a similar magical

Henri Rousseau, depicted in one of the self-taught painter's portrait-landscapes. DEA/M. Carrieri/De Agostini/Getty Images

quality. Less well known are what he called portrait-landscapes. In these the subject is painted surrounded by a scene or objects suitable to his occupation. Rousseau died in Paris on Sept. 2, 1910.

PETER PAUL RUBENS

(b. 1577–d. 1640)

Regarded for more than three centuries as the greatest of Flemish painters, Peter Paul Rubens was nearly as famous during his lifetime for his adroit achievements as a diplomat. The master artist of his day, he was learned in science and politics as well and spoke seven languages fluently. His charm made him welcome in the courts of Europe.

Rubens was born on June 28, 1577, at Siegen, in Westphalia, Germany. His father had settled there when he was exiled from Flanders. His mother took her children to Antwerp after her husband's death in 1587. In 1600 Rubens traveled to Italy, where he entered the service of the duke of Mantua. He studied the works of the great masters of Italian art. To the elements he absorbed he added his own individual sense of color and his boldness of design to create a style that left its mark on generations of painters who followed him.

Returning to Antwerp in 1608, he entered the diplomatic service of the Spanish rulers of Flanders. He was soon regarded as the leading Flemish artist. Among his masterpieces are *Le Coup de Lance* and *The Descent from the Cross*.

Rubens received so many orders for large paintings that he set up a huge studio. He usually only did the sketches for the composition, the principal figures, and the finishing strokes himself. The filling in was done by paid assistants and pupils. Another great Flemish painter, Anthony Van Dyck, was one of his students.

Rubens made long visits to foreign capitals both as a painter and as a diplomat. After having helped arrange the peace treaty of 1630 between Spain and England, he was knighted by Charles I of England.

Rubens married Isabella Brandt in 1609. In December 1630, four years after his first wife's death, he married 16-year-old Hélèna Fourment. Among his finest works are paintings of these women and their children. Rubens died in Antwerp on May 30, 1640.

GEORGES SEURAT

(b. 1859–d. 1891)

French neoimpressionist painter Georges Seurat is the ultimate example of the artist as scientist. He spent his life studying color theories and the effects of different linear structures. His 500 drawings alone establish Seurat as a great master, but he will be remembered for his technique called pointillism, or divisionism, which uses small dots or strokes of contrasting color to create subtle changes in form.

Georges-Pierre Seurat was born on Dec. 2, 1859, in Paris. He studied at the École des Beaux-Arts in 1878 and 1879. His teacher was a disciple of Jean-Auguste-Dominique Ingres. Young Seurat was strongly influenced by Rembrandt and Francisco de Goya.

After a year of military service at Brest, Seurat exhibited his drawing *Aman-Jean* at the official Salon in 1883. Panels from his painting *Bathing at Asnières* were refused by the Salon the next year, so Seurat and several other artists founded the Société des Artistes Indépendants. His famous canvas *Sunday Afternoon on the Island of the Grande Jatte* was the centerpiece of an exhibition in 1886. By then Seurat was spending his winters in Paris, drawing and producing one large painting each year, and his summers on France's northern coast. In his short life Seurat produced seven monumental paintings, 60 smaller ones, drawings, and sketchbooks. He kept his private life very secret, and not until his sudden death in Paris on March 29, 1891, did his friends learn of his mistress, who was the model for his painting *Young Woman Holding a Powder Puff.*

ALFRED STIEGLITZ

(b. 1864–d. 1946)

The first photographer to have his work exhibited in American art museums, Alfred Stieglitz was also a devoted supporter of modern art, particularly modern American art. The Photo-Secession group he founded in 1902 contributed to the acceptance of photography as an art form. The group's gallery, which opened in 1905, was officially named the Little Galleries of the Photo-Secession, but because it was located at 291 Fifth Avenue in New York City, it soon came to be referred to as 291. Stieglitz used the gallery to provide a showcase for many European and American artists, including August Rodin, Henri Matisse, Paul Cézanne, Pablo Picasso, Georgia O'Keeffe, John Marin, and Arthur Dove.

Stieglitz was born in Hoboken, N.J., on Jan. 1, 1864. He went to school in New York City until 1881, when the family moved to Europe. After studying mechanical engineering at the Berlin Polytechnic in Germany

for a few months in 1883, Stieglitz became interested in photography and decided to study photochemistry instead. He was responsible for notable technical innovations that allowed the taking of photographs in rain, in snow, and at night.

Stieglitz moved to the United States in 1890. Frustrated by public unwillingness to accept photography as an art form, he assembled a group of talented American photographers and founded the Photo-Secession. He was also largely responsible for the public recognition of contemporary American artists. One of the artists whose work was seen for the first time at 291 was Georgia O'Keeffe. She and Stieglitz were married in 1924. In addition to his other work, Stieglitz edited and published *Camera Work*. This magazine appeared between 1903 and 1917 and included beautifully reproduced photographs as well as articles that advanced the cause of serious photography.

After 291 closed in 1917, Stieglitz devoted more time to photography. In New York City and at his summer home in Lake George, N.Y., he created a famous series of photographic portraits of O'Keeffe and also a group of photographs of cloud patterns, whose abstract shapes suggest various emotions. Between 1925 and 1929 he opened two other galleries in New York City.

Stieglitz's prints were the first photographs to be received as works of art by major museums in Boston, Mass.; New York City; and Washington, D.C. He died on July 13, 1946, in New York City.

ANTONI TÀPIES

(b. 1923–d. 2012)

Antoni Tàpies was a Catalan artist, credited with introducing contemporary abstract painting into Spain. He began as a surrealist but developed into an abstract artist under the influence of French painting and achieved an international reputation.

Antoni Tàpies Puig, also known as marqués de Tàpies, was born on Dec. 13, 1923, in Barcelona, Spain. In 1943 Tàpies began studying for a law degree at the University of Barcelona, but he abandoned this career in 1946 to devote himself to painting. He was largely self-taught as an artist.

In 1948 he helped to found in Barcelona the Dau al Set ("Seven-Sided Die"), an organization of surrealist artists and writers influenced especially by Paul Klee and Joan Miró, which published an artistic-literary review. In 1950 he saw the work of Jean Dubuffet, which turned him away from surrealism and toward abstraction. Tàpies began in 1955 to work with a thick impasto, and these paintings, similar in their power and individuality to American abstract expressionist paintings, secured his world reputation. In his later works Tàpies began including real objects such as buckets, mirrors, and silk stockings in his paintings—and even larger objects, as in his assemblage *Desk and Straw*, in which an actual desk serves as the "canvas." His works of lithography were noted for their mysterious, spontaneous effects. He also collaborated with poet Joan Brossa on a number of illustrated books. He died on Feb. 6, 2012, in Barcelona.

In 1990 the Tàpies Foundation, which housed some 2,000 works by the artist, opened in Barcelona. He was elevated to the Spanish nobility in 2010 with the hereditary title Marqués de Tàpies.

BERTEL THORVALDSEN
(b. 1770–d. 1844)

Danish sculptor Bertel Thorvaldsen (also spelled Thorwaldsen), prominent in the Neoclassical period, was the first internationally acclaimed Danish artist. In the 20th-century reevaluation of Neoclassicism, however, Thorvaldsen's reputation outside Denmark declined. Thorvaldsen's most characteristic sculptures are reinterpretations of the figures or themes of Classical antiquity. The *Alexander* frieze of 1812 in the Palazzo del Quirinale in Rome, Italy—modeled in only three months in anticipation of a visit by Napoleon—is an example of the feverish energy with which Thorvaldsen could at times work. Religious sculptures include the colossal series of statues of *Christ and the Twelve Apostles* (1821–27) in the Vor Frue Kirke in Copenhagen. He also made numerous portrait busts of distinguished contemporaries.

Thorvaldsen was born Nov. 19, 1770, in Copenhagen, Denmark. He was the son of an Icelandic wood-carver who had settled in Denmark.

He studied at the Copenhagen Academy and won a traveling scholarship to Rome, where he was to live most of his life. The success of Thorvaldsen's model for a statue of *Jason* (1803) attracted the attention of the Italian sculptor Antonio Canova and launched Thorvaldsen on one of the most successful careers of the 19th century. When he returned to visit Copenhagen in 1819, his progress through Europe—in Berlin, Warsaw, and Vienna—was like a triumphal procession. His return to Denmark from Rome in 1838, when he eventually decided to settle in Copenhagen, was regarded as a national event in Danish history. A large portion of his fortune went to the endowment of a Neoclassical museum in Copenhagen (begun in 1839), designed to house his collection of works of art, the models for all his sculptures. By his own wish, Thorvaldsen was to be buried in the museum. He died March 24, 1844.

TITIAN

(b. 1488/90?–d. 1576)

One of the master painters of the Italian Renaissance was Titian, an artist of the Venetian school. He was born Tiziano Vecellio at Pieve di Cadore, north of Venice, and tradition says that as a boy he painted with juices extracted from flowers. When he was about 10 years old, he went to Venice. There he studied under Giovanni Bellini, the greatest Venetian painter of the day.

In 1513 Titian was made superintendent of public works. His duties included finishing great works begun by Bellini and painting a portrait of each doge, or ruler, of Venice who came into office. His good looks and courtly manners won him friendships in the highest circles. In 1530, after his wife died, he built a beautiful home and entertained famous artists and literary people. He died of old age on Aug. 27, 1576, during an epidemic of plague and was buried with honors in the church of Santa Maria de Frari.

Titian is considered among the greatest colorists of all time. Among his finest works were his portraits. He had a talent for capturing the personalities and the physical characteristics of his subjects. His first portrait of the Holy Roman Emperor Charles V led that ruler to make Titian a count and a Knight of the Golden Spur and to make Titian's children nobles.

Titian had a great respect for the beauty of the human form, and this, combined with his talent for creating rich, brilliant color, allowed him to depict many religious and mythological subjects equally well. He portrayed religious figures with a majestic dignity and elegance. His mythological scenes are alive with movement and often humor. He was especially sensitive to the grace and charm of women, as is evident in his nude figures.

Titian painted until his death, and a large number of his works have survived to the present time. Among the best known are *Assumption*, *Christ and the Pharisee*, *The Entombment of Christ*, *The Supper of Emmaus*, *The Holy Family (with a Worshiping Shepherd)*, *Christ Crowned with Thorns*, *Presentation of the Virgin in the Temple*, *Bacchus and Ariadne*, *Venus Anadyomene*, *The Rape of Europa*, and *The Vendramin Family*.

DIEGO VELÁZQUEZ

(b. 1599–d. 1660)

Spain's greatest painter was also one of the supreme artists of all time. A master of technique, highly individual in style, Diego Velázquez may have had a greater influence on European art than any other painter.

Diego Rodríguez de Silva Velázquez was born in Seville, Spain, presumably shortly before his baptism on June 6, 1599. His father was of noble Portuguese descent. In his teens he studied art with Francisco Pacheco, whose daughter he married. The young Velázquez once declared, "I would rather be the first painter of common things than second in higher art." He learned much from studying nature. After his marriage at the age of 19, Velázquez went to Madrid. When he was 24 he painted a portrait of Philip IV, who became his patron.

The artist made two visits to Italy. On his first, in 1629, he copied masterpieces in Venice and Rome. He returned to Italy 20 years later and

Statue honoring Diego Velázquez, Spain's premier painter, outside the Prado Museum in Madrid. parema/E+/Getty Images

bought many paintings—by Titian, Tintoretto, and Paolo Veronese—and statuary for the king's collection.

Except for these journeys, Velázquez lived in Madrid as court painter. His paintings include landscapes, mythological and religious subjects, and scenes from common life, called genre pictures. Most of them, however, are portraits of court notables that rank with the portraits painted by Titian and Anthony Van Dyck.

Duties of Velázquez's royal offices also occupied his time. He was eventually made chamberlain of the palace, and as such he was responsible for the royal quarters and for planning ceremonies.

In 1660 Velázquez had charge of his last and greatest ceremony—the wedding of the Infanta Maria Theresa to Louis XIV of France. This was a most elaborate affair. Worn out from these labors, Velázquez contracted a fever from which he died on August 6.

Velázquez was called the "noblest and most commanding man among the artists of his country." He was a master realist, and no painter has surpassed him in the ability to seize essential features and fix them on canvas with a few broad, sure strokes. "His men and women seem to breathe," it has been said; "his horses are full of action and his dogs of life."

Because of Velázquez's great skill in merging color, light, space, rhythm of line, and mass in such a way that all have equal value, he was known as "the painter's painter." Ever since he taught Bartolomé Murillo, Velázquez has directly or indirectly led painters to make original contributions to the development of art. Others who have been noticeably influenced by him are Francisco de Goya, Camille Corot, Gustave Courbet, Édouard Manet, and James McNeill Whistler. His famous paintings include *The Surrender of Breda*; an equestrian portrait of Philip IV; *The Spinners*; *Las Meninas*, or *The Maids of Honor*; *Pope Innocent X*; *Christ at Emmaus*; and a portrait of the Infanta Maria Theresa.

JOHANNES VERMEER

(b. 1632–d. 1675)

One of the greatest 17th-century Dutch painters, Johannes Vermeer is known for his light-drenched genre pictures—scenes from everyday life. They are both realistic and poetic, conveying the sense that Vermeer saw beauty in the simplest object.

Johannes, or Jan, Vermeer was baptized in Delft, the Netherlands, on Oct. 31, 1632. His father dealt in art, kept a tavern, and designed and sold *caffa*, a type of silk cloth. Nothing further is known of Vermeer's first 20 years. The marriage register at Delft records his wedding on April 5, 1653, to Catharina Bolnes. When he was 21, Vermeer was enrolled as a master painter in the Guild of St. Luke, which regulated the arts in Delft. Only a few of Vermeer's paintings were dated. The dates of his other works have been deduced mainly from the brush strokes, which grew progressively more refined. Working with painstaking care, Vermeer painted fewer than 40 pictures in his lifetime. The exact number is disputed. Like his father, he also dealt in art.

The exact date of Vermeer's death is not known, but he was buried at Delft on Dec. 15, 1675. At the time of his death, his finances were at their lowest. Staggering under defense taxes imposed after France declared war on the Netherlands in 1672, the Dutch no longer had money for art. Vermeer's widow petitioned the town council for a bankruptcy ruling. She struggled to keep her husband's work intact despite grasping creditors.

Nine years after Catharina died in 1687, there were 21 paintings by Vermeer listed in the catalog of an Amsterdam auction. This was the last time for nearly 200 years that his work received serious attention. In the mid-19th century artists began to recognize that he was unique in his understanding and rendering of light and shade. Characteristic of Vermeer's paintings are *Allegory of Painting* (1673); *Officer and Laughing Girl* (1658); *View of Delft* (1661); *Girl with the Red Hat* (1667); and *Young Woman with a Water Jug* (1665).

ÉLISABETH VIGÉE-LEBRUN

(b. 1755–d. 1842)

Among the most successful of all women artists was the French painter Élisabeth Vigée-Lebrun. She painted portraits of European society figures and of royalty, and she is especially noted for her portraits of women.

Marie-Louise-Élisabeth Vigée was born on April 16, 1755, in Paris, France. Her father was Louis Vigée, a portrait artist who became her first teacher. In 1776 she married an art dealer, J.-B.-P. Lebrun. Her great opportunity came in 1779, when she was summoned to the Versailles palace to paint a portrait of Queen Marie-Antoinette. The two women became friends, and over the next decade Vigée-Lebrun painted more than 20 portraits of Marie-Antoinette in a great variety of poses and costumes. She also painted a great number of self-portraits, in the style of various artists whose work she admired. In 1783, because of her friendship with the queen, Vigée-Lebrun was grudgingly accepted into the Royal Academy.

When the French Revolution broke out in 1789, Vigée-Lebrun left France. For 12 years she traveled in Italy, Austria, Germany, and Russia, painting portraits and playing a leading role in society. She returned to Paris in 1801 but disliked social life there during Napoleon's era. Vigée-Lebrun soon left for London, England, where she painted pictures of the royal court and of British Romantic poet Lord Byron. Later she went to Switzerland, where she painted a portrait of popular French-Swiss intellectual Madame de Staël. About 1810 Vigée-Lebrun moved back to Paris, where she continued to paint until her death.

Vigée-Lebrun was one of the most technically masterful portraitists of her era. Her pictures are notable for their freshness, charm, and sensitivity. During her career, by her own count, she painted 900 pictures, including some 600 portraits and about 200 landscapes. Vigée-Lebrun was a woman of much wit and charm. Her memoirs, *Souvenirs de ma vie* (1835–37; "Reminiscences of My Life"), are a lively account of her life and times. Vigée-Lebrun died on March 30, 1842, in Paris.

KARA WALKER

(b. 1969–)

Kara Walker is an American installation artist who used intricate cut-paper silhouettes, together with collage, drawing, painting, performance, film, video, shadow puppetry, light projection, and animation, to comment on power, race, and gender relations.

Walker was born Nov. 26, 1969, in Stockton, Calif. Her father, Larry Walker, was an artist and chair of the art department at the University of the Pacific in Stockton. She showed promise as an artist from a young age, but it was not until the family moved to Georgia when she was 13 that she began to focus on issues of race. Walker received a bachelor's degree (1991) from the Atlanta College of Art and a master's degree (1994) from the Rhode Island School of Design, where she began working in the silhouette form while exploring themes of slavery, violence, and sex found in sources such as books, films, and cartoons.

In 1994 Walker's work appeared in a new-talent show at the Drawing Center in New York. Her contribution was a 50-foot (15-meter) mural of life-size silhouettes depicting a set of disturbing scenes set in the antebellum American South. The piece was titled *Gone, an Historical Romance of a Civil War as It Occurred Between the Dusky Thighs of One Negress and Her Heart*. That work and subsequent others, such as a series of watercolors titled *Negress Notes (Brown Follies)* (1996–97), caused a stir. Some African American artists, particularly those who participated in the civil rights movement, deplored her use of racist caricatures. Walker made it clear that her intent as an artist was not to create pleasing images or to raise questions with easy answers. She also explained her use of the silhouette by stating that "the silhouette says a lot with very little information, but that's also what the stereotype does."

In 1997, at age 27, Walker received a John D. and Catherine T. MacArthur Foundation "genius grant." Her work was exhibited in galleries and museums worldwide, and she served as the U.S. representative to the 2002 São Paulo Biennial. She was also on the faculty of the School of the Arts at Columbia University in New York City.

In 2006 the Metropolitan Museum of Art in New York City featured her exhibition titled "After the Deluge," which was inspired in part by the devastation wreaked the previous year by Hurricane Katrina in New Orleans. The exhibition juxtaposed pieces from the museum's own collection—many of which depicted black figures or images demonstrating the terrific power of water—with some of her own works. The intermingled disparate images created an amalgam of new meaning fraught with a discomfiting ambiguity characteristic of much of Walker's output. Two subsequent major exhibitions were "My Complement, My Enemy, My Oppressor, My Love," a comprehensive traveling show organized in 2007 by the Walker Art Center in Minneapolis, Minnesota, and "Rise Up Ye Mighty Race!" (2013) for the Art Institute of Chicago.

ANDY WARHOL

(b. 1928?–d. 1987)

Pop art, according to its practitioners, is meant to create art that is indistinguishable from life. According to Andy Warhol, one of its most innovative producers, it is intended to bore the audience and to indicate the dehumanization of modern life. The creators of pop art

Andy Warhol, sandwiched between two of his pieces in his New York City studio near the start of his pop-art career. Mondadori/Getty Images

have taken pleasure, if not pride, in exalting the commonplace and the commercial in the technological society of the late 20th century.

Andy Warhol gained his early fame by such things as repetitive paintings of Campbell's Soup cans and sculptures of Brillo soap pad cartons. He mass-produced his art in a workshop called the Factory by means of a photographic silk-screen process that allows endless reduplication of an image. He followed these with variations of celebrity portraits in garish colors. One of his best-known works is a portrait of actress Marilyn Monroe, described by a critic as a woman "carefully manufactured, packaged, and sold like a can of soup."

Although a celebrity, Warhol was always a bit vague about his early years. He was born Andrew Warhola about 1928, probably somewhere in Pennsylvania. Philadelphia, Pittsburgh, and McKeesport have been suggested as likely places. He studied art at the Carnegie Institute of Technology and worked as a window decorator in Pittsburgh. In the early 1950s he moved to New York City and became a commercial artist. In 1957 he won the Art Directors' Club Medal for a giant shoe advertisement. His notoriety in the art world began in 1962, when he exhibited his paintings of soup cans.

After commercial success with his art, he turned to filmmaking, producing a series of apparently meaningless movies in which nothing happened. *Empire* (1964), for instance, simply focused on the Empire State Building for eight hours. He later added a semblance of plot in *The Chelsea Girls* (1966) and *Blue Movie* (1969). In 1968 he was shot and nearly killed by an actress he had once hired. After recovering he continued filming and published some of his work in book form, including *Andy Warhol's Exposures* (1980). Warhol died on Feb. 22, 1987, in New York City.

JAMES ABBOTT McNEILL WHISTLER

(b. 1834–d. 1903)

"If silicon had been a gas, I might have become a general in the United States Army," remarked James Abbott McNeill Whistler years after he had become a world-famous painter and etcher. Whistler, who was born in Lowell, Mass., to an old military family in 1834, entered the United States Military Academy at West Point when he was 17. He liked to draw and neglected his other studies. He was dismissed from West Point after proving in an examination that he was too hazy about identifying chemical elements.

Whistler worked as a draftsman for the Coast Survey in Washington, D.C., where he learned the technique of etching. In 1855 he sailed for Europe and never returned to the United States. He studied in Paris for two years under Charles Gleyre.

Emphasizing the analogy between color and music, Whistler borrowed musical terms to describe his pictures, calling them nocturnes, arrangements, symphonies, and harmonies. He called the famous portrait of his mother, for instance, *Arrangement in Grey and Black*. Although the terms are now accepted, critics then laughed at Whistler. During his life he was more noted for wranglings with critics and for sharp satirical wit than for his work as a painter.

In his individual way Whistler was a follower of the French impressionist movement and was much influenced by Japanese prints and by Gustave Courbet. He avoided brilliant colors, and his pictures are characterized by an absence of detail. His nocturnes usually depict moonlit scenes on water with lights shining dimly through mist. In 1877 the critic John Ruskin wrote about *Nocturne in Black and Gold: The Falling Rocket*, for which Whistler asked 200 guineas, "I never expected to hear a coxcomb ask 200 guineas for flinging a pot of paint in the public's face." Because of this criticism Whistler sued Ruskin for libel and received one farthing for damages. The expenses of the lawsuit led to bankruptcy, but Whistler flaunted the coin on his watch chain ever after.

Whistler was also known as a graphic artist, producing about 400 etchings and dry points and nearly 150 excellent lithographs. This versatile genius also wrote several witty books. Whistler died in London on July 17, 1903.

GLOSSARY

abstract expressionism An artistic movement of the mid-20th century comprising diverse styles and techniques and emphasizing especially an artist's liberty to convey attitudes and emotions through nontraditional and usually nonrepresentational means.

Baroque Of, relating to, or having the characteristics of a style of artistic expression prevalent especially in the 17th century that is marked generally by use of complex forms, bold ornamentation, and the juxtaposition of contrasting elements often conveying a sense of drama, movement, and tension.

cartoon Originally, a full-size drawing used for transferring a design to a painting, tapestry, or other large work; since the 19th century, a humorous or animated drawing or parody.

cubism A style of art that stresses abstract structure at the expense of other pictorial elements especially by displaying several aspects of the same object simultaneously and by fragmenting the form of depicted objects.

dadism A movement in art and literature based on deliberate irrationality and negation of traditional artistic values.

draftsman An artist who excels in drawing.

fauvism A movement in painting typified by the work of Matisse and characterized by vivid colors, free treatment of form, and a resulting vibrant and decorative effect.

gisant A recumbent sculpture of a deceased person shown usually with arms crossed over the chest.

impasto The thick application of a pigment to a canvas or panel in painting; also, the body of pigment so applied.

impressionism A style of painting that began in France around 1870 that uses spots of color to show the effects of different kinds of light, and that attempts to capture the feeling of a scene rather than specific details.

lithography The process of printing from a plane surface (as a smooth stone or metal plate) on which the image to be printed is ink-receptive and the blank area ink-repellent.

GLOSSARY

Mannerism An art style in late 16th century Europe characterized by spatial incongruity and excessive elongation of the human figures.

nihilistic Of or relating to the belief that traditional morals, ideas, beliefs, etc., have no worth or value.

phenomenology A philosophical movement originating in the 20th century, the primary objective of which is the direct investigation and description of phenomena as consciously experienced, without theories about their causal explanation and as free as possible from unexamined preconceptions and presuppositions.

pictorialist Of or relating to an approach to photography that emphasizes beauty of subject matter, tonality, and composition rather than the documentation of reality.

pointillism The theory or practice in art of applying small strokes or dots of color to a surface so that from a distance they blend together.

realism The theory or practice of fidelity in art and literature to nature or to real life and to accurate representation without idealization.

Salon Official exhibition of art sponsored by the French government.

stucco A fine plaster used in decoration and ornamentation (as of interior walls).

surrealism The principles, ideals, or practice of producing fantastic or incongruous imagery or effects in art, literature, film, or theater by means of unnatural or irrational juxtapositions and combinations.

tenebrism A style of painting especially associated with the Italian painter Caravaggio and his followers in which most of the figures are engulfed in shadow but some are dramatically illuminated by a beam of light usually from an identifiable source.

transept The part of a cruciform church that crosses at right angles to the greatest length between the nave and the apse or choir.

The Metropolitan Museum of Art
1000 Fifth Avenue
New York, NY 10028-0198
(212) 535-7710
Web site: http://www.metmuseum.org
The Metropolitan Museum of Art houses a sweeping collection of
   paintings, sculptures, photographs, artifacts, and more, represent-
   ing movements from around the world from the past and present.
   The museum's libraries and study centers offer a wealth of information on all aspects of art to researchers and the public.

Montreal Museum of Fine Arts
P.O. Box 3000, Station "H"
Montreal, QC H3G 2T9
Canada
(514) 285-2000
Web site: http://www.mbam.qc.ca/en
The Montreal Museum of Fine Arts houses paintings, sculptures, prints,
   photographs, drawings, artifacts, and more, from antiquity to the
   present day. Activities for students and families, lectures, courses,
   and more are also available to the public.

The Museum of Modern Art (MoMA)
11 West 53 Street
New York, NY 10019
(212) 708-9400
Web site: http://www.moma.org
One of the world's preeminent museums, the MoMA has a number of
   seminal works of modern and contemporary art. Its many resources
   and programs include lectures, courses, and workshops for teachers,
   students, and the public at large.

National Gallery of Art
6th and Constitution Avenue NW
Washington, DC 20565
(202) 737-4215

Web site: http://www.nga.gov/content/ngaweb.html

Art from the Renaissance to the present day is preserved in the National Gallery of Art's extensive collection and is available for free viewing. The gallery also offers lectures, films, workshops, and concerts to the public and conducts research in the field of art through its research institute.

National Gallery of Canada
380 Sussex Drive
P.O. Box 427, Station A
Ottawa, ON K1N 9N4
Canada
(613) 990-1985
Web site: http://www.gallery.ca/en/

With a collection of art from around the world as well as from Canada itself, the National Gallery of Canada allows visitors to view both regional and world-renowned masterpieces. Activities for students and families are also offered.

WEB SITES

Due to the changing nature of Internet links, Rosen Educational Services has developed an online list of Web sites related to the subject of this book. This site is updated regularly. Please use this link to access the list:

http://www.rosenlinks.com/pysk/artist

FOR FURTHER READING

Bird, Michael. *100 Ideas That Changed Art*. London, England: Laurence King Publishers, 2012.

D'alleva, Anne. *Look! The Fundamentals of Art History*. London, England: Pearson Publishing, 2010.

Leonardo Da Vinci, Irma A.Richter (ed.), Martin Kemp, and Thereza Wells. *Leonardo da Vinci: Notebooks*. New York, NY: Oxford University Press, 2008.

Dempsey, Amy. *Styles, Schools and Movements*. London, England: Thames and Hudson, 2011.

Gerlings, Charlotte. *Great Artists*. New York, NY: Rosen, 2012.

Gompertz, Will. *What Are You Looking At? The Surprising, Shocking, and Sometimes Strange Story of 150 Years of Modern Art*. New York, NY: Penguin, 2012.

Osborne, Richard (ed), Dan Sturgis, and Natalie Turner. *Art Theory For Beginners*. Danbury, CT: For Beginners, 2009.

Rackza, Bob. *Name That Style: All About Isms in Art*. Minneapolis, MN: Lerner, 2009.

Shipps, Steve. *(Re)Thinking "Art": A Guide for Beginners*. Hoboken, NJ: Wiley-Blackwell, 2008.

Updike, John, and Christopher Carduff (ed.). *Always Looking: Essays on Art*. New York, NY: Knopf, 2012.

INDEX